ALSO AVAILABLE BY

Stephen Rich Merriman

Anger and Rage Addiction &
The Self-Pact: New Lights on an Old Nemesis

Pathfinding Through Multiple Personality

The Living Oracle: Wisdom &
Divination for Everyday Life

Outside Time: My Friendship with Wilbur

Who's 'At Home' in Your Body (When You're Not)?

When You Lose What You Can't Live Without

(ed.) Speak But the Word:
From Multiple Personalities to Wholeness

Behavioral Addictions:

A New Solution to Very Old Problems

Behavioral Addictions:

A New Solution to Very Old Problems

Stephen Rich Merriman, PH.D.

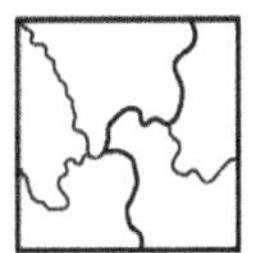

Four Rivers Press

Amherst, Massachusetts

fourriverspress.com

Book design by James McDonald
JAMESMCDONALDBOOKS.COM

Printed in various locations worldwide

ISBN 978-0-9817698-7-5
Library of Congress Control Number: 2015917859

Library of Congress subject headings:

1. Substance-Related Disorders – complications. 2. Diagnosis, Differential.
3. Self-destructive behavior. 4. Behavior, Addictive – psychology.
5. Behavior, Addictive – prevention & control 6. Addicts – Treatment.
7. Behavior, Addictive – rehabilitation 8. Spirituality.

Behavioral Addictions: A New Solution to
Very Old Problems is dedicated to

Emily Sara Taylor Merriman

an ever-true spirit and soulmate on the
adventurous path of self-discovery

Contents

Acknowledgments

A book is rarely, if ever, the product of a single person's work and efforts.

I wish to thank my wife, along with loyal friends and colleagues, who have supported my authorial efforts over these many years, both as readers and loving, constructive critics of my work. First and foremost I express my enduring love and gratitude to my spouse and partner Emily Merriman, my most fearless critic and unstinting supporter of my efforts, for the quality of her engagement in the process of sculpting this book. Her contributions have helped to make this work more readily accessible than would otherwise have been the case.

From my list of loyal friends and colleagues I wish to thank John McKey Hallowell (recently departed), Anne Allison, Johnn O'Sullivan, Gloria Horvitz, Bill Ryan, Jeanne Lightfoot, and Mark Solomon for their words of encouragement and general enthusiasm for what has found its way onto these pages.

I also wish to thank the New England Institute of Addiction Studies (www.neias.org) and especially Denise Adams, Administrative Director of NEIAS. The Institute, which sponsors an annual addiction studies summer school, decided in 2005 to offer a course on Behavioral Addictions. This was a far-reaching initiative on the part of NEIAS, for, at that time, there was little recognition of the relevance of Behavioral Addictions in the overall terrain of addictions diagnosis and treatment. In the decade since, it has been my great good fortune to have served as the instructor for the "Introduction to Behavioral Addictions" course at the school.

In recent years, gauged by the response to this course, the field of addictions diagnosis and treatment is awakening to the importance of including this range of addiction manifestations under the umbrella of what an "addictions treatment field" needs to address and codify as a part of its professional mission. For this I am exceedingly grateful—and hopeful.

It is this increasing recognition of the reality and relevance of Behavioral Addictions that has provided me the motivation to expand the course notes into the book you are now holding.

In addition to the gratitude I have expressed to those previously mentioned, please know that I am also grateful to you, the reader, for your interest in Behavioral Addictions. I hope that you will find this book to be helpful to you, both personally (if needed) and professionally (to the ongoing benefit of many others).

—S.R.M.

Preface

To my dear readers—those of you who are recovering addiction-prone people, your friends, families, partners and other loved ones, addiction treatment professionals, still-"active" alcoholics and drug addicts, and all those whose lives have been affected, at some level, by the scourge of addiction:

It is an honor to present this book to you. This book reflects forthrightly and as accurately as possible the fruits of over forty years of immersion in the realm of Behavioral Addictions (as well as substance-based ones). This odyssey was lived out, initially, in the arena of personal travail, and then took the form of my working, for a number of years, as staff psychologist in an addictions treatment hospital and then a community mental health center. This was followed, over the next twenty-five years, by my laboring as a CADAC and then an LADC 1 (as formal credentialing started to arise within the profession[1]) in a private practice setting.

Over that time, what arose at first as a kind of impossible puzzle with, seemingly, lots of missing pieces gradually revealed itself as a context in which, as my comprehension incrementally increased, additional pieces of the puzzle began

1. The CADAC (Certified Alcohol and Drug Addiction Counselor) came into being in 1984 or so. It was issued by the Massachusetts Committee for Voluntary Certification of Alcoholism Counselors, Inc. In the early 1990s I served on the board of directors for this organization. The LADC I is the top-level clinical license offered by the Commonwealth of Massachusetts. It was first issued in 2004.

to appear and assemble themselves in more whole and complete ways. What started, all those years ago, as the tease of a puzzle, gradually deepened to become a field of knowledge and grounded experience—Behavioral Addictions—the pieces of the puzzle having long-since been set in place.

My hope is that those of you who travel a bit of the journey reported in these pages may discover, within yourself, a resonance that will ring true to you about what is presented here, and what its relevance is to you and others to whom it may become your privilege to be of assistance. Perhaps, within these pages, you may also discover answers to questions which, in some way, you've "felt," but haven't had the words to express, nor known how to ask.

This book aims to be helpful to two different (but not necessarily unrelated) readerships. The first consists of those who are in recovery from various addictions—most likely alcohol- and drug-related, and who are finding themselves, notwithstanding their earnest efforts in recovery, still beset by various troublesome—often "compulsive"—behaviors and their damaging effects on the quality of life.

If you are in this group, this book may provide a larger context for gaining a comprehension of what you're up against as a "recovering"—but still afflicted—alcoholic or drug addict, along with some clarity regarding what the healing path ahead may hold for you by way of challenges and possibilities.

For those of you who work in the addictions treatment field (or other human services arenas)—many of you (I well know) having already come through your own personal-life torments—you will discover within these pages awarenesses, and lines of approach, that can contribute to your effectiveness as a human services professional. Those of you who are addictions treatment professionals will find explicit and detailed diagnostic criteria for Behavioral Addictions, along with perspectives on treatment for these conditions. These perspectives are pragmatic, and can be readily utilized in your work setting. In addition to diagnostic and treatment considerations, *this book implicitly issues a call for the professional field of addictions treatment to enlarge its sense of vision as to what an "addictions treatment field" really needs to address.*

It is with a full heart—and, at my age, gratitude for still having a pulse (!)—that I offer this work to you. May you all find it useful, and may *you* expand upon it in ways that can be of true, grounded help to others in need of these fruits, born of decades-long experience—both in theory and practice—in the diagnosis and treatment of Behavioral Addictions.

I wish you all many blessings as you continue on your own life's journey, in whatever capacity—non-professional, professional, or both—to which this contribution may be of assistance.

Yours, with the appropriate love of a seasoned professional and fellow traveler,

—Stephen Rich Merriman, PH.D.
Mount Pollux Summit, Amherst, Massachusetts
—Looking towards Stratton Mountain, Vermont
(within "hailing distance" of Manchester and East Dorset)—
visible, 70 miles to the NNW, on a sparkling autumn day!
October 15th, 2015

CHAPTER ONE

Early Intimations (Someone 'Noticed')

IT IS A TRUTH in the addictions treatment field that the origins of professional focus—whether it be the diagnosis and treatment of alcoholism, drug addiction and/or, more recently, professional concerns with gambling, sex, "love," anger and rage—have their roots in grassroots, self-help, mutual-aid initiatives. In the field of alcoholism and drug addiction treatment, most models of professionalized treatment have their origins in the mutual-help fellowships Alcoholics Anonymous, (founded in Akron, Ohio in 1935) and Narcotics Anonymous (founded in Los Angeles, California in 1953).

For those early, stalwart, recovering grassroots pioneers who got sober and clean in A.A. and N.A. all those decades ago, "recovery," in the form of A.A.'s "Twelve Steps" became an accessible, palpable reality, arising from the rough and tumble of adversity, desperation, despair, and hope.

Those brave souls who navigated the path to whatever recovery might be attainable to them placed great stock in A.A.'s "Big Book" (*Alcoholics Anonymous*, originally published by Works Publishing, NYC, 1939).[2] In terms of what *was*

---

2. A.A.'s "Big Book," *Alcoholics Anonymous* is readily consultable online: http://www.aa.org/pages/en_US/alcoholics-anonymous

attainable, the beautiful and uplifting sentiments expressed in the "Promises," set forth on pages 83–84 of that book seemed to portend numerous positive outcomes for those who got "clean and sober," maintained a vital connection to A.A. (and/or N.A.) as a whole, and dedicated themselves to "working the Steps" as a way of life.[3] Those wonderful promises were presented as being realized to a significant degree at the point of a recovering person's completion of the first nine of the Twelve Steps of recovery.

Bill W., the primary author of A.A.'s "Big Book," was a visionary. In enshrining the Promises within the progression of the Twelve Steps, he was attempting to encompass the largest and broadest scope of recovery that he could envision. However, at the time he wrote the Promises (around 1937) he, himself, was sober no more than two and a half years. This length of sobriety was no mean feat, given the morass that late-stage alcoholism had lead him into, but . . . from the standpoint of long-term recovery—meaning what longer-term sobriety actually held, and yielded—two and a half years'

3. For those of you who don't have a copy of *Alcoholics Anonymous* by your elbow, the Promises can easily be consulted online: http://www.sonoma-countyaa.org/resources/aa-meeting-resources/downloads/The_Promises.pdf
4. This fact of Bill W.'s relatively short length of sobriety at the time he wrote the Promises takes not one whit away from the magnificence of his achievement. There are far too few visionaries in the world who have anything to peddle other than smoke and mirrors. Bill W.'s grand vision was a real statement of the underlying redemptive potential of healing energy, notwithstanding the chronological limitations of what he could know, or had witnessed, when he set pencil to paper.

worth of sobriety was lacking in what could only be arrived at by experientially-based *knowing*. Bill W.'s Promises could only be, at that early time, with so much sober experience yet to be lived out, "Bill W.'s earnest hopes."[4]

It is here that the story takes a bit of a shift away from the seemingly assured outcome of "living one's way into happy destiny"—being "happy, joyous and free."

What started to transpire, over time, on a number of occasions, was this: A small subset of sober and clean, recovering (in terms of alcoholism and drug addiction) individuals among those early grassroots pioneers began to notice that certain of their behaviors carried eerie hallmarks of their earlier behavior as active alcoholics and drug addicts. At the level of individual awareness, *someone noticed.*

Here is what these early, intrepid observers of their own behavior, noticed:

> (1) They noticed that they were engaging in certain behaviors to enhance pleasure (as do we all), reduce pain (as do we all), remain functional and/or ward-off symptoms, either physical, psychological, or both, of withdrawal or deprivation.
>
> (2) They noticed that they were requiring, over time, increasing levels of absorption and immersion into indulgence activities in order to achieve the desired effects of indulging. In other words, they noticed that they were developing *tolerance* to what they were craving, which required greater *intensity* of active engagement to breach so that a "payoff" moment could be reached.

> (3) They realized that they were experiencing loss of control over the rate, frequency and duration of their behavioral indulgences:
>
> RATE = how much "xyz behavior" they were doing during any given episode.
>
> FREQUENCY = how often indulgence episodes would occur.
>
> DURATION = how long (temporally) an indulgence episode would last.
>
> (4) They noticed that when they were separated or cut-off from their "source of supply"—the means and opportunities to indulge and act out—they would experience symptoms, either physical, psychological, or both, of withdrawal, that could erupt in any dimension of human experience: mind, body, spirit and heart.
>
> (5) They recognized that levels of unmanageability—a negative quality they thought they had left far behind them when they had gotten sober and clean in terms of alcohol and drugs, were back—unbidden, unsought, not knowingly cultivated or desired. Negative consequences of an increasingly troublesome nature had returned.

In hindsight, the evidence that these five awarenesses were taking root across a range of behaviors is obvious: Twelve Step-oriented fellowships based on the model pioneered by Alcoholics

Anonymous, but seeking to address issues other than alcoholism, started to come into being. Without an upwelling of awareness—without someone "noticing"—such mutual aid fellowships could not, and would not, have come into existence.

Here is a sample of what started to arise on the "grassroots" side:

(1) Gamblers Anonymous (GA), started in Los Angeles in 1957, addressing problems of "compulsive gambling" in all its forms (sports betting, lotteries, day trading, commodities futures and options trading, casino gambling, off-track betting, etc.). "Compulsive Gambling" was the first out-and-out behavioral—non-substance-based—addiction to begin (very gradually) to come to societal recognition, primarily through the consciousness-raising that has its roots, once again, in the initiatives of a self help fellowship.

(2) Overeaters Anonymous (OA), founded in Los Angeles in 1960, addressing compulsive overeating—arguably a "hybrid" addiction involving both behaviors and substances (binge foods, etc.).

(3) Debtors Anonymous (DA), which formally emerged in New York City in 1976, addressing compulsive spending and indebtedness.

(4) Sex and Love Addicts Anonymous (SLAA), started in the Metro-Boston (Massachusetts) area in 1976, addressing areas of addictive sexual behavior and "love" addiction—i.e. such experiences as "falling in love with falling in love," getting "high" on "emotional intrigue,"

and morbid dependency on an "other." [5] [6]

Independent of self-help, mutual aid initiatives, there were also some early awarenesses as to the existence of Behavioral Addictions that started to surface from the professional side. During this period (1970s–1980s) these observations arose from among the ranks of human services professionals and other researchers who functioned outside the realm of the addictions treatment field. This era ushered in a small wave of offerings that gave evidence that, though few and far between, a small number of hardy professionals were starting to "notice" that certain behaviors presented as "addictive"—as worthy of

---

5. Other "S" fellowships that started during this period included Sexaholics Anonymous, Sexual Compulsives Anonymous and Sex Addicts Anonymous.

6. Unlike the areas of alcoholism and drug addiction, in which grassroots self-help initiatives (A.A. and N.A., respectively) helped pave the way for the emergence of the professionalized field of alcoholism and substance abuse/drug addiction treatment, the professional community was largely blind to what these subsequent grassroots movements in Behavioral Addictions were empirically pointing to: *the need for the addictions treatment field to expand its sense of vision as to what an "addictions treatment field" really needed to consider and address as a part of its professional calling and mission.* In fact, for several decades following the inception of these behaviorally-aimed self-help initiatives (all of those mentioned having survived and grown in the meantime), the addictions treatment field remained stuck and entrenched, considering itself to be dealing solely with alcoholism and chemical dependency, and continually defaulting into referring others with "symptoms of co-morbidity" (often behavioral addictions) into the non-addiction-savvy realm of "mental health" practitioners. Given what, at the grassroots level, was staring the addictions treatment field in the face, this was a remarkable under-reaching—a pathetic default by the field on advocating for, and claiming, its rightful territory of concern *and treatment.*

being considered addictions unto themselves. Here are three examples:

(1) *Love and Addiction,* by Stanton Peele and Archie Brodsky. This book, published in 1975, helped to identify a series of interpersonal dynamics that the authors felt constituted something akin to addiction (although their descriptions sound, at times, a lot like what, in years to come, would be seen more as co-dependency). Their book is descriptive, even diagnostic, but not prescriptive. Still, their book was a wake-up call, and is historically important.

(2) Another work, *How to Break Your Addiction to a Person,* by Howard Halpern (published in 1982) was hands-on and pro-active in its approach: the first prescriptive (in the manner of self-applied) treatment book, if you will, for "love" addiction (in the form of morbid dependency).

(3) I well recall encountering, in the spring of 1978, a feature article that appeared in the monthly periodical *Psychology Today.*[7] The article was reporting on a study of long distance running. Much of the piece discussed research findings regarding how world-class runners adopt either *dis*sociative or *as*sociative approaches to dealing with the challenges (usually involving the need to cope with intense pain) that are often encountered in the course of long runs. What really got my attention was the mention, near the end of the article, that, especially

---

7. "The Mind of the Marathoner," by William P. Morgan (*Psychology Today,* April, 1978/VOL. 11, NO. 11.).

with the *dis*sociative strategy, running becomes a kind of "trip," which can include hallucinations, out-of-body experiences, likening running, as an activity, to a kind of "wonder drug" for producing a "high" that is often followed by "a state of total quiescence and relaxation that can last for hours." The report noted, with concern, that to maintain the occurrence of such states required increasing the length and intensity of runs. The article then went further into describing the "exercise addict" as a person who "cannot exist without exercise, whatever the cost." It noted that injured runners, in pursuit of the high, forced themselves, against medical advice, to continue to run, risking compounding their existing injury; they would also become so absorbed in their running that they would withdraw from family and friends. The article noted, poignantly, that "the beginning jogger should be warned that quest for a 'breakthrough' or a 'transcendent experience' can produce addiction and psychological trauma."

As far as I know this report in *Psychology Today* was the first account of addiction to running, and, more generally, addiction to exercise, or (if you will) addiction to what later would be described as endorphin release.[8]

---

8. The *Psychology Today* article was liberally cited in a subsequent article, entitled "Marching to Euphoria," by William Oscar Johnson (*Sports Illustrated*, July 14th, 1980 issue). This article generalized the concept of running addiction into "exercise addiction," reported compellingly on the lengths that some runners were willing to go to achieve a regular dose of "runners high" (transcendence via running), and related findings that spoke to the shattering (to the point of concerted suicidal ideation) qualities of withdrawal some runners experienced when, for health or other reasons, they were forced to stop. The article is also noteworthy for its mention (for the first time that I'm aware of) of endorphins as a possible causative feature in

gaining a "high" through exercise. Endorphins as a possible factor in addictions were just starting to be considered in the late 1970s. Of course, the field of neurochemistry (notably an understanding of the action of serotonin and dopamine), and the study of endorphins, has come a long way in the decades since this article was published. Nevertheless, the generic endorphin concept has much to commend it as a common bridge between both substance-based and purely behavioral addictions. Understood in these terms, Behavioral Addictions, like substance-based addictions, are unleashed via a "substance." Those who would later claim that even Behavioral Addictions at some level involve "substances"—psychoactive compounds—are correct. The difference is that endorphins are endogenous—both produced and released within the body (endorphin = "endogenous morphine"). In other words, the distinction in Behavioral Addictions is that the compounds put in play are entirely created and consumed within the body, rather than administered or ingested (in some fashion) from "outside." The addiction, in all such cases, becomes, in addition to the inner experiences that accompany endorphin release (along with the action of other endogenous neurotransmitters), *also* an addiction to the outer world behaviors which, when pursued with sufficient vehemence and intensity, result in the release of these endogenous compounds. The "Marching to Euphoria" article is quite difficult to locate and access online. Yet, it is so seminal to the study of Behavioral Addictions that, despite the ungainly URL that connects to it, I include it here: http://www.si.com/vault/1980/07/14/824802/marching-to-euphoria-in-pursuit-of-an-elusive-feeling-of-well-being--even-invincibility--some-unsuspecting-runners-may-actually-have-turned-into-addicts-and-the-monkey-on-their-backs-is-wearing-jogging-shoes

CHAPTER TWO

Operative Definitions: The Five Diagnostic Criteria—*Making the Connection between Alcohol- and Substance-based Addictions and Behavioral Addictions*

IT IS TIME TO RETURN to what those early recovery pioneers noticed about some of their non-substance-based behaviors while they were in the process of getting, *and being,* sober and clean in terms of alcohol and other mind-altering compounds. In returning to the five basic awarenesses those early pioneers achieved regarding certain of their non-substance-based behaviors, it may prove helpful to present their discoveries in a more formal, profound way.

So . . . here are those five (5) awarenesses—which we'll henceforth refer to as the *Five Diagnostic Criteria*—more concisely formulated and presented. Each one represents a criterion for addiction, *although all five (5) criteria must be present for an addiction—either chemical-based or behavioral—to be conclusively diagnosed.*

Criteria for Addiction: The Five Diagnostic Criteria

(derived directly from alcoholism and drug addiction, and applicable for diagnosing all addictions, whether substance-based or purely behavioral)

(1) Use of a substance or an activity for the purpose of enhancing pleasure (either physical or psychological, or both) or decreasing pain (either physical, psychological, or both)—energizing, or sedating—OR for the purpose of maintaining the ability to function (a tolerance-related effect). (Note: key words for this criterion: Pleasure, Pain, and Ability to Function)

(2) Over time, there is an *increasing* amount of *consumption* or *indulgence* required to achieve an acceptable level of "pay-off," or return—the development of Tolerance.[9] (Note: key words for this criterion: Increasing Consumption/Indulgence, Tolerance)

(3) *Loss of control* over rate, frequency and/or duration of consumption/indulgence.

RATE = how much "quantity" I'm doing when I indulge/act out

FREQUENCY = how often I'm acting out/indulging

DURATION = how long (temporally) an indulgence/acting out episode lasts

(Note: key phrase for this criterion: Loss [of] Control)

9. For a fuller discussion of Tolerance, consult Appendix One on page 132.

(4) *Symptoms of withdrawal* (physical, psychological, emotional, spiritual, or any combination of the above) are encountered if consumption/indulgence, and access to "source of supply"/opportunities-to-act-out, are abruptly curtailed (another tolerance-related effect).
(Note: key phrase for this criterion: Withdrawal Symptoms)

(5) *Progression: increasingly negative consequences* accruing over time as a direct or indirect result of loss of control—life unmanageability.
(Note: key words for this criterion: Progression, Negative Consequences, Life Unmanageability)

These are the Five Diagnostic Criteria for *any* specific addiction. These criteria are derived entirely from the realms of alcoholism and drug addiction and discovered to be operative, as well, across a range of non-alcohol/non-substance-based behaviors. Once again: *All the Five Diagnostic Criteria must be present for any addiction to be conclusively diagnosed.* If even one of the criteria is absent, it's *not* addiction (at least in terms of what can be conclusively diagnosed and—as necessary—defended).

Let's take the Five Diagnostic Criteria and cast them in two different ways. The first way is in a single sentence constructed as an *objective* statement. This is an attempt to capture what addiction "looks like" as viewed objectively—*as observed from the outside* by an external observer. Here is the objective definition of addiction:

> Addiction is the use of a substance or an activity for the purpose of enhancing pleasure or decreasing pain—energizing or sedating—OR to maintain the ability to function, by a person who needs, over time, more "quantity" of the rate, frequency and duration of indulgence episodes, who also experiences symptoms of physical, mental, emotional and/or spiritual withdrawal if cut of from his/her source of supply or opportunity to indulge, and whose life becomes progressively unmanageable as the pattern of usage continues.

The second way we'll cast the Five Diagnostic Criteria is as a *subjective* definition of addiction. The subjective definition is an attempt to present an impression of what addiction *feels* like—*as something that is experienced on the "inside"* (at least by someone who is becoming aware of it, rather than being blindly and unknowingly driven by it—and therefore being in denial about it). Here is the subjective definition of addiction:

> Addiction is the exploitation of ***me*** by a substance or activity, which enslaves me through pleasure enhancement, pain elimination—energizing or sedating—OR by providing me the capacity to remain functioning, in which the substance or activity forces itself upon me at an increasing rate, frequency and duration which I am unable to resist, causes me to experience symptoms of physical, mental, emotional and spiritual withdrawal if I attempt to turn my attention and allegiance away from the substance or activity, resulting in the cost, to me, of the progressive deterioration of my life.

CHAPTER THREE

The BIG NEWS!!

ONCE WE RECOGNIZE that the dynamics of addiction (The Five Diagnostic Criteria for correct diagnosis) exist in non-substance-based realms as they do in substance-based ones, we can no longer consider addiction as something peremptorily reducible to merely having "an" addiction to this (particular) substance, or that (particular) behavior. *As a phenomenon that clearly bridges and transcends both the purely substance-based realm and the purely behavioral realm, we are obliged to acknowledge that addiction is, first and foremost, an . . .*

. . . *ENERGY!!*

While is takes but a moment to verbally express this concept (this chapter presenting it is, indeed, very short), the significance of this awareness—and the reality underlying it—can not be overstated. Everything that follows in this book is based upon it. To those of you who may be feeling somewhat startled by the concept of addiction being, at its roots, an underlying *energy* which can manifest in innumerable areas of human endeavor and behavior, I ask that, before you read any further in this book, you stop at the end of this chapter . . . and reflect deeply on this notion. In so doing, you can discover if the Addiction Energy concept holds any degree of resonance for you, both in terms of what you have witnessed in others or, perhaps, grappled with within yourself. There is a lot of information yet to be presented and discussed about Addiction Energy, but none of it will be worth much in the absence of some underlying resonance with the concept having being established.

As you may already have sensed, Addiction Energy is an *encompassing, unifying* concept. It is inclusive of all addictions and their outer-world manifestations. As we shall see, the umbrella of addiction is broad, indeed, and welcomes a whole range of behaviors to claim their rightful place under its canopy.

The Addiction Energy concept also demystifies the apparent stark differences between various addictions—differences that are habitually used to diagnostically set such behaviors apart from one another as "co-occurring," "co-morbid" syndromes, or "disorders," complete with pathology labels applied from the *Diagnostic and Statistical Manual* nomenclature of the mental health professions (a typical phenomenon whenever the addictions treatment world bumps up against the "mental health" treatment world). However, with the presence of the Five Diagnostic Criteria, these "co-morbid" syndromes, on further discovery, so often turn out to be additional manifestations of addiction, which, due to the Addiction Energy that underlies and fuels them, means that *they are all related to one another.* Because of the common denominator of Addiction Energy and, therefore, the interrelationship that runs through all of them, they are, when approached in this way, more consistently and cohesively treatable.

One further point: As an encompassing, inclusive concept, Addiction Energy is clearly a different animal from the splintering of human behavioral syndromes into the myriad diagnostic categories of the *Diagnostic and Statistical Manual* (*DSM*), and the specialization-run-amok in the credentialing and treatment arenas that has resulted from this tendency towards hyper-categorization.[10] This joining together of a circle of substance-based and non-substance-based behaviors under the single heading "Addiction" forms a *natural* assemblage because *all* of these behaviors (in those who are afflicted by one or more of them) share the same Five Diagnostic Criteria.

Each behavior, in its addiction-laden outworking, forms one channel through which Addiction Energy establishes its domain in both the sufferer's (addict's, individual's) inner

10. To be fair, the tendency to hyper-categorization is not limited to the mental health and addictions treatment fields, although it is certainly in evidence there. The expansion of diagnoses into the "run amok" stage is everywhere in evidence in the human services fields, and especially in the field of general medicine. As of 10/01/15, diagnostic codes required for physician reimbursement of services expanded from approximately 14,000 to over 70,000. New diagnoses include such gems as "Underdosing of Caffeine," "Problems in Relationships with In-laws," and "Other Contact with a Squirrel." It's enough to make one wonder how many different shades of "Obsessive Compulsive Disorder" have been identified (*among* the ranks of the "categorizers"). (http://www.marketwatch.com/story/doctors-brace-for-70000-insurance-codes-2015-09-28).

world and, through "acting out" behavior, in the outer world, as well. This recognition, as it may come to awareness in the therapist, counselor, clinician, patient, client, and/or oneself, contributes to more hopeful outcomes, overall, in dealing with addictions, for in coming to terms, however successfully, with any one of them, the stage is set for being able to subsequently address others that may, over the course of recovery, come into the foreground.

Treating any addiction, whether in oneself of others, has everything to do with learning about the dynamics of what Addiction Energy is, and how it works. Based on the application of this knowledge and awareness, any relative success in addressing any specific addiction becomes a transferable skill that can be brought to bear on those that remain and become problematic. The *dynamics* of Addiction Energy, regardless of the channels through which it may gain expression, are constants across the board.

In the following chapter we will begin to take a closer look at what the qualities and dynamics of Addiction Energy are, and how they operate.

CHAPTER FOUR

Addiction Energy: What Is It?

Qualities and Characteristics: *Traditional & Non-Traditional Manifestations of the Energy—*

"Addiction Energy" is a very broad concept. What are the characteristics and qualities of Addiction Energy? There are many components that contribute to, and, collectively, comprise, it. To gain an appreciation of the scope of Addiction Energy's workings, it is necessary to take a closer look at some of its constituent qualities and capabilities. Only by carefully considering the broad range of its characteristics can it become possible to start to construct lines of approach to influencing it. Short of this, one is left with adopting stopgap measures that have little if any staying power, for they are employed in the absence of a fuller understanding of the dynamics they are ostensibly attempting to alter.

The following compendium of qualities does not purport to be a complete aggregation of Addiction Energy's constituent parts and tendencies, but it covers a sizable swath of what it consists of—and is capable of. For those of you familiar with addiction—whether in the realm of personal experience, in bearing witness to the sufferings of others in one's personal life, or in one's professional capacity (or all three)—a number of these qualities will strike an instant note of recognition. Other qualities to be described, however, are likely to be unfamiliar to you, and, quite possibly, may even be a bit surprising.

DISPLACEMENT (A)

Let's start by considering a—maybe *the*—hallmark quality of Addiction Energy. This characteristic, or quality, is called: Displacement (an old psychoanalytic term). In the addiction realm, displacement is the ability of Addiction Energy to manifest in many different ways, including the use of substance-based and non-substance activities. Addiction Energy can seek, co-opt, and utilize, potentially *any* channel of manifestation in the outer world, whether substance-based or non-substance-based, through which to discharge. For Addiction Energy, any channel, or outlet, can be made to suffice.

PHYSICAL COMPULSION (B)

One of the original qualities recognized by early A.A.s, physical compulsion is an inner itch, a body-centered attraction: craving. Once triggered—and it can be triggered either when an addiction-prone person is in a state of deprivation, or as a reaction to an initial indulgence (building on itself)—physical craving hungers to get the inner itch scratched: to fill an inner emptiness which, through the very act of sating it by an indulgence or a behavior, will temporarily null out the hunger . . .

all the while making the inner void with its attendant craving *larger.*

Note: One of the earlier concepts of what was operative in alcoholism was that the alcoholic has an "allergy" of the body regarding the presence of alcohol, which results in an allergic reaction in the form of the triggering of physical compulsion.

MENTAL OBSESSION (C)

Another seminal concept having its origins, vis-à-vis alcoholism, in early A.A., mental obsession is usually taken to be a narrowing down of the mental focus to a single strident, unrelenting fixation that comes to dominate conscious intention and functioning. However, mental obsession can also function more subtly, as a *less conscious*, or even *unconscious* phenomenon—taking, for instance, the form of a vague desire, or a seemingly non-specific gravitational pull. In these forms, mental obsession lulls and lures, rather than coerces—it is seductive, rather than merely imperious. This form of obsession is all the more dangerous than the more blatant forms of obsession, because, as a manifestation of Addiction Energy working behind the scenes, it is much more difficult to identify and, in some fashion, contain.

It is worth noting that mental obsession always has a delusional, distortional quality to it. The "object" of one's desire and quest seems to enlarge—to expand—to occupy the whole field of consciousness, when what is *actually* occurring is that consciousness is becoming narrower and narrower as it focuses more and more intently on achieving its aim. This narrowing of consciousness gives the illusion—and provides the *subjective* experience—that the object of its quest is *enlarging.*

POSSESSION (D)

This quality, unto itself, is not usually recognized as being germane to understanding, diagnosing and treating Addiction. Curiously, though, during the Spiritualist Movement in mid-nineteenth century America, the terms "obsession" and "possession" were often used interchangeably, so in a colloquial (and thoroughly subjective and non-professional) sense, there was some recognition of overlapping qualities denoted by these two terms. If we take possession as a generic concept that has its roots in any number of religions and cultures—both ancient and modern—it can be useful to us as we try to gain an understanding of Addiction Energy to consider possession's qualities and dynamics.

Possession is an energy that feels foreign or alien. It is also an energy that is capable of using us, *without our necessarily being aware of it*—as its *host*—to achieve its own ends, without its paying any regard to what we would consider to be our best interests. Possession is also an energy that seems to have a "psychic" component to it—an uncanny quality in which temptation and opportunity for indulgence and acting out have a way of showing up, of ambling into possibility, at just the wrong moment—undermining, or corrupting, one's own conscious resolve and force of will.[11]

---

11. A close reading of the "Step One" chapter in the Alcoholics Anonymous

ATTACHMENT (E)

Attachment is one of the prevailing characteristics of Addiction Energy. Addiction Energy has a need to attach to other life forms. Part of the energy of attachment is to be constantly looking and scanning for opportunities to do so.

Attachment is a *generic* quality of all life on earth (and presumably elsewhere, as well). In terms of human history, the concept of attachment is central to Buddhist thought, and *that* tradition has its origins over 2500 years ago. In Buddhist philosophy, the centrality and pitfalls of *misdirected* attachment-seeking is clearly recognized as central to human suffering. This pervasive problem of humankind is articulated as a (maybe *the*) major challenge confronting human awareness and existence. The valuable concept of problematic attachment gives rise to certain questions and observations pertinent to the understanding of addiction. Here are a small handful of them:

(1) Is the basic energy of addiction—the *ENERGY!!*—sourced as a kind of primordial urge—in the very impetus to exist at all? . . . or, perhaps more specifically, to exist as a space-time embodied form in the period of historical time in which we find ourselves functioning in this lifetime?

---

book *Twelve Steps and Twelve Traditions* (originally published in 1953) indicates that A.A.'s founders and "old timers" were taken up with the relevance of the "possession question." For a summary of some of the evidence supporting this conclusion, please consult Appendix Two on page 135. *Twelve Steps and Twelve Traditions* (nicknamed the *Twelve & Twelve)* is readily consultable online at http://www.aa.org/pages/en_US/twelve-steps-and-twelve-traditions.

(2) If so, *are striving, desire and attachment, however ill-conceived they may be, inseparable from life itself?*

(3) If the answer to the prior questions is "yes," and true, *is the tendency to addiction an inalienable feature of life itself—a "given" to the human condition?*

(4) Here, in succinct form, are Buddhist philosophy's contributions to identifying and addressing such possibilities: The First Noble Truth of Buddhism is "Life is Suffering." The Second Noble Truth of Buddhism is "The Cause of Suffering is Craving/Desire." The Third Noble Truth of Buddhism (this is a hopeful one) is "Alleviation of Suffering is possible through 'awakening.'" (The Fourth Noble Truth of Buddhism is a presentation of the "Eight-Fold Path" through which awakening, and freedom from attachment—and therefore from suffering—become attainable.)

Note: So, in terms of Buddhist philosophy, notwithstanding the "baked-in-the-cake" pervasiveness of attachment in the form of misplaced hunger that informs, and maybe, in its fundaments, even gives rise to, the drama of human existence . . . there is hope for finding a liberation from its shackles, and, therefore, from addiction.

'ROUSABLE'/TRIGGERABLE (F)

Addiction Energy is capable of rousing itself (of becoming "roused") into desire, hunger, craving and indulgence on a moment's notice, or . . . more likely, *without any prior notice.*

It is always capable of triggering into activation for possible outflow and discharge—whether substance-based or behavioral. This quality of Addiction Energy can "show up" anywhere and anytime—seizing on potentially any plane of human endeavor.

The neurology of triggering is faster than thought. It takes seventy milliseconds (70ms—1/14th of a second) for a human being to trigger—whether into a state of fight, flight, freeze, desire, or craving—and by the time "reason," or "awareness" knows that this is happening . . . *it has already happened.* It's old news. Triggering already occurred four hundred-thirty milliseconds (430ms—nearly half a second) earlier.[12] Lamentably, "reason," and the neurology that supports it, are slower neurological processes than the neurology of triggering. *Reason—and conscious intention—cannot keep up with "triggering."* This inescapable reality points to the futility of relying on rational understanding alone to counter the triggering of craving and acting-out behaviors.

DIS-EASE (G)
(Holistic notion)

This quality of Addiction Energy is akin to the buildup of electrical charge in a cumulonimbus thunderhead cloud. The buildup of charge constitutes an imbalance that seeks to become neutralized through a discharge of its pent-up charge, or energy. There is something about Addiction Energy that is

12. The neurological/synaptic network response data source for this data can be found at: http://plato.stanford.edu/entries/consciousness-temporal/emperical-findings.html

chronically, as punctuated by "acutely," out of whack—imbalanced. It is an energy of disarray—lopsided, with only *primitive* (impulsive, untamed) means through which to attain even a moment's worth of stability or equilibrium. On the psychological/emotional/spiritual/physical planes, this state of being continually out of balance with itself creates a chronic tension. When tension builds to a flash point, the energy is impelled to neutralize itself. It seeks to be equalized, brought into alignment, switched, "released," and, however ephemerally, integrated by some means.

MANIA (H)

(Pressing urgency: self-justification and rationalization run wild)

Within the throes of this quality of Addiction Energy (figuratively a case of obsession on steroids), nothing seems more imperative, more necessary, more correct, more fulfilling, more compelling, more whole, more complete, more *crucial* than what is happening in the immersion of momentary indulgence. "There is nothing I want more than what is happening in this moment." "This is what I most truly want." "I *must* have this drink; I *must* have this drug." "I *must* have this experience." "I *must* have this ___________ (person, thing). "I *must* have this ___________ (*whatever . . .*)."

DESPERATION (I)

(Panicky, reactive clutching and stampeding)

Desperation is an aspect of Addiction Energy that has the potential—and capability—of *instantly* creating an addictive experience out of any substance or activity with which it comes into contact—anything that can supply a moment of "relief."

This quality of Addiction Energy is like a primeval urge, a determining component of character and personality formation, often (although not always) having its roots in a background of childhood physical abuse/sadism, childhood sexual abuse, childhood emotional abuse and/or emotional/physical neglect, deprivation and physical or emotional starvation.

SEDUCTION/SEDUCTIVE (J)

(The teasing "come on"—with serious intent)

This aspect of Addiction Energy is a quality that is ever seeking to lull and lure its victim (or host) into "trying something"—thereby providing a pathway through which the *ENERGY!!* can find expression, an outlet, or discharge. This quality carries the ambience of "I am innocent; I won't hurt you." "This one's free; it's 'on me,' and no one else ever has to know." "I'm beautiful—and hungry—and I'm yours, and I can give you a great ride—a great high, and you'll be fine." "I'll never betray you." "You can tarry with me to your heart's (and body's) content, and come to no harm."[13] "Come on . . . I know

13. If "Seduction" practiced a truth-in-advertising standard while hawking its

you're hungry, and you know you want me; now's your chance." This quality perfuses the air with an aroma of irresistibility and inevitability combined. Once "I" cave in, succumbing to its beguilements and blandishments—once I am seduced—Addiction Energy (in this case, the quality of "seduction") starts to work through me, and "I" may become seductive.

OPPORTUNISTIC/OPPORTUNISM (K)
(Viral)

This quality of Addiction Energy is always scanning for weakness and vulnerability—a way to gain a toe hold, then a foothold, and pry open an entrance where, once "inside," it can develop a stronghold. It sets up shop, takes over and comes to run the show. Its activity, in probing for weakness and susceptibility—a "way in"—is incessant. It is ever operative; it never ceases. Sometimes this quality of Addiction Energy appears to have a psychic component which can manifest in the form of psychic phenomena related to gaining access to other peoples' vulnerability—or suddenly finding oneself in vulnerable circumstances where one is at risk of being corrupted.

SELF-LOATHING/SELF-HATRED (L)

The qualities of self-loathing/self-hatred reside deep within Addiction Energy. Sometimes, as Addiction Energy is roiling

---

wares, instead of the vibe of "You can tarry with me to your heart's (and body's) content, and come to no harm," it would state, rather, "You can tarry with me to your heart's (and body's) content, and come to *know* harm."

around an addict's neurology, they may be experienced directly, as an apparent confirmation of the "deepest truths" one has been taught about oneself in childhood: that one is worthy only of being despised and hated. When these "subjective truths" that one has been taught are held inwards and not projected, acts of self-mutilation, self-mortification, self-slashing and disfigurement (any of which can lead to endorphin-based "highs") are often features of the acting-out palate. More often, though, the self-loathing and self-hatred are less directly experienced by ego consciousness. Rather, self-loathing and self-hatred are projected onto the outer world, which is seen to consist of an unending procession of assholes, ignoramuses, egotists, narcissists and morons. Again, these projections are often the outworkings of internalized messages received—and uncritically accepted—about oneself as a consequence of growing up in a toxic, damaged family. Vitality, that basic life-energy, has been twisted, contorted and distended into discharges of self-destructive behavior towards "hated" others. Each destructive act, originating as an inner explosion of stringent judgment and disdain, supplies a "negative rush" experience which, in its negativity-based intensity, is self-confirming.

THE NEGATIVE RUSH (M)

The Negative Rush is one of the deepest underlying qualities present in Addiction Energy. The Negative Rush embodies the energy of raw, destructive intention that "gets off" on itself. It relishes rage for the sake of rage, destructiveness for the sake of destructiveness, self-hatred for the sake of self-hatred, bloodlust for the sake bloodlust, vengeance for the sake of vengeance, sadism for the sake of sadism, cruelty for the sake of cruelty, oppression for the sake of oppression.

As a sickening "downer," the Negative Rush delivers doses of adrenalin and self-reviling which build on each another, leading to cumulative, upwelling unleashings of more and greater destructive acts. *The churning cauldron of rage and fury that lace up the action feeds on itself.*

The Negative Rush does not know any kind of introspective logic (as in, for instance, having some awareness of personal wrongdoing combined with a simultaneous need to deny taking any personal responsibility for it), nor has it conscience, as might manifest in the forms of guilt and remorse, as moderating influences. *It requires no moral justification for its actions.* Rather, within the Negative Rush, experiences of emotion that seem like guilt and remorse are, when they arise, *conscience-less,* and serve more sinister intentions. Within the context of the Negative Rush such emotion serves only to amp up self-loathing and hatred to ever higher pitches—"highs"—of destructive fury.

Of all the qualities of Addiction Energy, this one—the Negative Rush—may be the most deep-seated, having taken on a life of its own in the early history of infancy and toddlerhood. At its depths, it underlies many (and perhaps all) of the multifarious issuances of Addiction Energy—the many "forms" that addiction—both substance-based and purely behavioral—can take.

METASTASIS (N)

Of all the qualities of Addiction Energy, this one is the most virulent. This quality of Addiction Energy is at the other end of the continuum from Displacement. If Displacement is the tendency, or characteristic, of Addiction Energy to pop-up in unexpected ways and places—often far-removed from an addiction that may have been already recognized and dealt with, the quality of Metastasis is different, more robust, and rampaging. In this manifestation of Addiction Energy, the original specific manifestation, or form, of acting out does *not* necessarily go underground, with its energy reappearing elsewhere. Rather, manifestations of active addiction continue to spread from venue to venue—quite possibly in a mélange of substance-based and non-substance-based activities. A person becomes engulfed by an ever-increasing circle of indulgence areas that, collectively, are, *all of them simultaneously,* channels of expression and discharge for Addiction Energy. If a metastatic cancer is often one that has been detected too late in the game to be readily treatable with any real hope of a healing outcome, so too, metastatic addiction is one that has taken root, spread, and enveloped, the soul and substance of an untreated, addicted individual over an extended period of time. There is, in such a case, a negative synergy of inter-linking between the various channels through which Addiction Energy is flowing. This juggernaut is very hard to penetrate by way of attempting to influence it. It constitutes a "late-innings" reality in untreated addiction. The prognosis for a person who is shackled to such a long, undiagnosed and untreated *pattern* of addiction is guarded.

VITALITY/"ELAN VITAL" (O)

We now come to one of the deepest, far-reaching and, perhaps, most *unsuspected* facets of Addiction Energy. Although vitality is the last quality on the list that we will be considering here, Addiction Energy certainly has additional qualities yet to be discovered and perused (and maybe pursued?). There's a lot of trail yet to "break" out there regarding components of Addiction Energy that warrant further exploration.

Thus far the traits of Addiction Energy that we have considered have had an ominous tone to them. They have each delineated a path to an addict's (along with our own—at least for those of us who are addiction-prone) undoing and demise. What a fantastic range of capabilities these qualities cover! From destruction for the sake of destruction and all the spiritual, mental, emotional and physical violence they push into our world, to the more subtle (but no less destructive) exploitive caresses of seduction and opportunistic scanning, at first glance these traits, collectively, depict an underlying energy—*ENERGY!!*—that either can't, generally, be resisted and thwarted, or is, in itself, almost entirely irresistible in its allure.

So . . . now we come to this apparently positive quality termed VITALITY. What can we say about this quality?

VITALITY is a quality that underlies all the negative outworkings of Addiction Energy. If we strip away every one of the apparently negative traits that comprise and shape Addiction Energy, there is, at the root (and heart) of the matter, only one residue left: *pure ENERGY.* Pure *ENERGY* is all that remains, and all we're left with. Pure *ENERGY* underlies *everything!*

Pure ENERGY is raw, untamed, instinctual. It is the very energy of life, always pressing for some form of manifestation—for having an embodied (whether as animal, vegetable or mineral) space-time life and existence. It may also seek manifestation on other planes of existence of which we, in human form, are unaware.

As a constituent of life, pure ENERGY exists as a basic resource, *in itself of neutral moral or ethical valence.* The seeds of the "all that is" which, from the human perspective, we would consider, value, and come to label as "Good," or "Evil" (and everything else in between) are contained, as a potential, within it. Here's the rub: without this basic Energy, life itself, in any form, would not be possible.

What are we to make of this quality of Addiction Energy? Can VITALITY in any way run counter to destructive forces that make up so much of the other aspects of Addiction Energy? Stay tuned. We will consider this matter presently.

CHAPTER FIVE

Specific Behavioral Addictions and Their Manifestations

As you may have concluded, based on our discussion in the previous chapter of the range of qualities that contribute to it, Addiction Energy is a remarkable energy indeed. Such a range of qualities, facets and characteristics give evidence of just what a fearsome foe, in its unredeemed state, Addiction Energy truly is.

In the absence of taking a full account of what is "in play" in Addiction Energy itself, we are left flailing in the dark as to what might constitute cures, remedies and strategic countermeasures for each of the qualities we have considered. Each of these fifteen qualities has something to contribute to our understanding of just was it is, in the addiction realm, that we are truly dealing with. Presently, we shall consider what may be drawn from each quality by way of implying possible lines of approach to influencing Addiction Energy to minimize its more harmful capabilities. However, before we consider "healing" lines of approach more fully, it is time to set forth a list of some of the behavioral areas through which Addiction Energy—the *ENERGY!!*—can issue and flow.

NOTE: *No single behavior on the following list is, in and unto itself, intrinsically addictive. Any specific behavior becomes addictive—"Addiction"—only when the Energy of Addiction has seized upon it as a channel for exploitation and discharge.* Once this happens, the Five Diagnostic Criteria for Addiction will start to show up in the specific behavioral area that has been "taken over." Once the Five Diagnostic Criteria are present, a basis for correct diagnosis of a Behavioral Addiction—and subsequent treatment approaches to influence it—are there to be noted and embarked on.

The range of behaviors that can be seized upon to serve as outlets for Addiction Energy is limitless. It naturally follows that *no complete list of Behavioral Addictions can ever be formulated.* The best we can do is to set forth a representative list of areas of behavior in which Addiction Energy can, and does, romp.

So here we go:

BEHAVIORAL ADDICTIONS
(incomplete list)

Key (Qualities of Indulgence):[14]

1 Central to the experience is the *narrowing focus of attention into a compressed (often visual) space.*
2 Central to the experience is *adrenalin rush—arousal.*
3 Central to the experience is *sedation—sedative effects.*
4 Central to the experience is *the illusion of having—or being able to acquire and exert—control.*

14. Please note: "The Key" for "Qualities of Indulgence" (1, 2, 3, 4, respectively) is included both at the beginning and at the end of the Behavioral Addictions list.

LABEL	EXAMPLES	QUALITIES OF INDULGENCE
1 Gambling	sports, commodity/financial futures, state lotteries, scratch tickets, casino gambling/slots, race tracks, day-trading, fantasy sports, card/board games, games of chance. "It's not whether I win or lose that matters; it's all about being 'in the *action*.'" Increasing tie-ins with video gaming. (See 5, below)	1, 2
2 Eating	bulimia, anorexia nervosa, imagined (obsessional) dysmorphia, sometimes sleepwalking (i.e., to the fridge for a late-night binge, with subsequent amnesia about the episode). Self-medicating.	3, 4
3 Internet	absorption, including Twitter, social networking (Facebook, etc.), YouTube, pornography, chat rooms, dating/"hooking up" sites, identity invention.	1, 2, 3[15], 4
4 Cell phone use, especially text messaging/instant messaging	need to be connected at all time. If I'm out of range, or unreachable, I experience acute anxiety—symptoms of withdrawal. Being "connected" becomes the most important activity, moment to moment,	1, 3, 4

15. Regarding the "2, 3" combination, sometimes the only way to get to the sedation effect, or payoff, is if it is preceded by an adrenalin/arousal stage, as in 3, 7, 8, 11, 12, 13, 15, 16, 17, 18, 19, 20, 21, 28, 29, 31, 32, 33. In truth, the sequence of a high state of energizing/arousal leading to a state of profound sedation/relief of tension is often, in combination, the overall payoff of an addiction experience.

4 Cell phone use, *Cont.*	in my life. With cell-phone technology linking to the greater internet, all the range of internet activities are portable and available, 24/7. Being "connected" places everything else, including attending to school, significant other, work responsibilities, etc., in a secondary role. Technology is what "reaches" the individual; actual in-person human encounters no longer get through. (See 31, below.)	1, 3, 4
5 Video games and gaming	absorption into a circumscribed universe where one has power—sex, violence, objectification and commodification of human attributes (elimination of "personhood"), mayhem. Increasing tie-ins with gambling. (See 1, above.)	1, 2, 4
6 Sex	runs a range from solitary acts (compulsive masturbation, voyeurism) to acts involving others (promiscuity, exhibitionism, bondage & discipline [role playing], "swinging," etc.); attendant risk of sexually transmitted diseases (HIV, HEP C, et al); complete objectification of human beings as "bodies," plumbing and "functions."	1, 3, 4
7 "Love," attachment hunger	runs a range from solitary experiences: fantasies crushes & secret passions, to experiences involving third parties, including: morbid co-dependency, "falling in love with falling in love," getting high on emotional intensity, inability to extricate	1, 2, 3, 4

	oneself from abusive relationships, the stifling entropy of "closed energy" interpersonal dynamics with partner(s), engaging in romantic intrigue behavior to maintain "source of supply." Emotional intensity is mistakenly taken as "being in love."	
8 Exercise	in all forms: chasing the endorphin high; excessive exertion to the point of self-injury, then placing one's health in further jeopardy by exercising against medical advice (in order to avoid feeling symptoms of emotional withdrawal—depression); frequently combined with use of steroids, the reliance on which often constitutes an addiction in itself.	2, 3, 4
9 Physical fitness	"iron man" triathlons, extreme workouts, etc. Issues of being attractive and "in control" of body—chasing the "perfect body": the perfect image of femaleness or manhood; creating an exoskeleton of muscle as impervious as possible to the experiencing and expressing of strong feelings and emotions (especially crying), usually combined with being *walled-off/sealed off from the emotional experience of life and living.*	2, 4
10 Pet	hoarding pets (often under the pretense of "rescuing" them)—to their detriment and the environment's; interacting with the pets one has to the exclusion of other relationships.	3, 4

11 Hobbies (of all stripes)	high levels of immersion and absorption; carry potential for addiction due to "screen" (computer, radio dial, aquarium tank, etc.) phenomenon: compressing a "universe" into a confined space. Collecting (stamps, coins, baseball cards, license plates, beer cans—anything: "The next addition to my collection completes it; this will make me *forever* satisfied *(for the moment!)*." Like any other manifestation of Addiction Energy, hobbies can come to take precedence over real-world responsibilities and satisfactions; living one's life at a "remove"—a form of "living life by proxy," immersion in a controllable fantasy world—being "around" one's life without really participating in it or being present to it.	1, 2, 3, 4
12 Creativity/ talent/"genius"	having an artistic gift which one comes to identify with as a personal possession; "serving the gift" becomes the priority, and all else comes second, third, fourth . . . nth . . . . Those moments when the artist is "seized by the muse," possessed by an imperious urge to create, and creativity *flows,* provide an exalted high that is difficult to surpass: life-purpose realized (on steroids!). In fallow interludes between creative bursts, depression (withdrawal) takes over. The "artiste" expects, and demands, that other people in his life honor him or her for his or her "gift," and orient their lives to support his or her talent and "genius." No sacrifice is too great if it serves "the gift!" Creativity, as corralled by Addiction Energy, becomes	1, 2, 3, 4

	polluted with egoistic self-serving and ever greater demands—hunger, craving—for recognition and adoration. The addiction-riddled artist is, always, a "legend in his own mind." Those around a person addicted to his "gift" suffer greatly if they "buy in" to living in the reflected glory of the artist's shtick, including the myth of the artist's "noble suffering" on behalf of his art. In the life of the artist addiction has plenty of camouflage to hide behind as it rampages, glorified in the folklore of "what it is to be an artist"—to be living an unconventional, libertine, and often tragic, down-and-out life. Ultimately, Addiction Energy distends, through personal dissipation, the content of what an artist creates through his or her art.	
13 Work	narrow plane of endeavor where one is validated, effective, or otherwise hides out. "Workaholism" creates a noble impression of being "dedicated to my job," while it actually is an act of evading being "present" to family, society and life in general.	1, 2, 3, 4
14 $ Indebtedness/spending	adrenal surge of "taking the plunge," followed by profound sense of relief from having done so—having "relieved the suspense." Feeling entitled to be among the "haves," and therefore having the right to spend the way the well-heeled do: "If I spend like them, I *am* like them" (at least until the bills come due).	2, 3

15 Conspicuous consumption	competing (by display) for "who's doing better," "who's more successful," or "who's winning"; projecting—and protecting—the image of being "successful."	1, 2, 3
16 Thrill-seeking, arousal-seeking, sensation-seeking, intensity-seeking, "adrenalin-junkie" behaviors	sky-diving, hang gliding, rock climbing, big wave surfing, bungee/base jumping, spelunking, "extreme sports," "joy-riding," shop-lifting and stealing, computer hacking, courting danger, dare-devil behaviors of all sorts. Pursuing the illusion that one is only "truly alive" when engulfed in and by risky, thrill-seeking, adrenalin-pumping, extreme (often life-endangering) experiences.	1, 2, 3
17 Shoplifting	tremendous sense of entitlement: "I deserve to have this." "Sticking it to 'the man,'" "getting over" on the "System." Adrenalin rush, need to "get away with something," to be smarter than, to be caught and punished—to suffer public disgrace, censure and humiliation; the rush of being shamed.	1, 2, 3, 4
18 Dare-devil behavior	"Tempting the fates." The thrill of being out of control—of courting death—of "thumbing one's nose at fate." Defying the odds. Taking risks to prove (to oneself) that I am "truly a man,"or "truly a woman," rather than a coward.	2, 3

19 Transcendence-seeking	meditation, yoga, isolation, "vision quests," shamanic drumming and dancing, sweat lodges, etc.; turning down (or up) the "volume"/intensity of an immersion experience to transcend one's identity and one's own experience of reality.	1, 2, 3
20 Therapy/healing modalities/regimens (psychological, emotional, spiritual, physical nutritional. mainstream, alternative therapies, etc.)	"I never met a therapy I didn't like (or could resist)." Each one is the next "big thing"—the one that is going to be the "final answer," the "big breakthrough"—the one that will finally "deliver me," "make me whole." "I *have* to try this." This behavior is essentially a variation of generic sensation/arousal seeking, and is an *avoidance* of facing, *inwardly*, what really needs to be addressed and dealt with. (It turns out that there is no such thing as deliverance, or redemption, "on the cheap.")	2, 3
21 Anger/rage	Triggering, immersion in the "negative rush," "rage for order," assertion of manhood or womanhood, vicious circles of shame and violence (emotional and [often] physical), amnesia (partial or complete) often following an episode/indulgence. Reactive experience of being hi-jacked into, or ambushed by, an episode. "Crimes of passion." "Living in the recoil, at the mercy of my own reactivity"—one's own triggering neurology. Contrition, shame, guilt and remorse are "reloading" activities, leading to the next unleashing, rather than a genuine penance. One of the most powerful and destructive of all the Behavioral Addictions.	1, 2, 3, 4

22 Power & influence-seeking	power-seeking/influence-seeking/manipulative behaviors (both active & passive)—one of the most pervasive of all the Behavioral Addictions.	2, 4
23 Self-hatred/self-destructiveness	the "negative rush." "I feel vile." "I'm a piece of shit; I've always been a piece of shit; I will always be a piece of shit." "I 'get off' on hating myself, and seeing how my hatred drags the people who love me down, compounding their misery and my misery, and confirming what a sick piece of shit I am."	1, 2, 3, 4
24 Security-seeking	profoundly truncated life due to preoccupation with security-seeking concerns and measures. Incessant attempts to guarantee *absolute* security and inviolability for oneself and significant others, often combined with a sense of having an increased scope of personal power—a "high" from finding, and employing, the "latest" in security-oriented hardware and software. There is even the hope that attempts will be made to penetrate, or defeat, one's *own* security systems and protocols (both hardware and software-based), which can lead to experiences of vindictive (though passive) triumph—or smug self-satisfaction—over successfully repelling and foiling attempted incursions by external, hostile forces. Perversely, those who have an addiction to security-seeking may develop finely honed skills for gaining entrance to, "cracking," hacking, or otherwise compromising, both "secure" physical	3, 4

	environments (as in safes, compounds and domiciles), as well as personal computers and digital networks.[16]	
25 Attention-seeking	conspicuous dressing/posturing for the purpose of being noticed. Developing the "currency" for making social impact.	2, 4
26 Isolation	opposite of attention-seeking. Leads to absorption into fantasy life, which is experienced as being enthralling and riveting. The "inner world" comes to hold more fascination and, at times, greater subjective rewards than the external world, leading to a profound disconnect from	3, 4

16. At first glance, some of what manifests as addiction to security seeking may seem to fit the criteria for obsessive-compulsive disorder (OCD). However, from the Behavioral Addictions side, a few distinctions may help clarify salient differences. First, in manifestations of OCD there is no obvious "payoff," in an energizing or de-energizing (as in "getting mellow") sense for the repetitive behaviors that are in evidence. They are all aimed at warding off negative consequences of some sort. There is no "high" to this, nor a previous history of developmental "highs" in the OCD pattern. The second point is that in later-stage addiction, the "action" in indulging (via either chemical compounds or acting-out behaviors), becomes, due to the effects of *tolerance*, entirely one of warding off withdrawal symptoms. The "highs" of usages and indulgences, while prominent earlier in the development of the addiction, are now long gone, and remaining "functional" by keeping withdrawal at bay—and away—is the main goal. So . . . it is true that later-stage addiction may resemble OCD, but, as previously stated, the developmental stages of an addiction (which include the "getting high" experiences) are different from the developmental track of OCD (in which such "payoff" experiences are absent). For more on the phenomenon *tolerance*, please consult Appendix One ("About Tolerance") on page 132.

	external reality, including attending to self-care (personal hygiene, seeking appropriate medical help, social connection, etc.). (See 29, below.)	
27 Self-mutilation, self-disfigurement	body piercing, cutting, behaviors increasing the likelihood of self-injury, all of which are used to focus extreme pain, *and* to achieve sedating, endorphin-related effects. These self-harm behaviors are consistent with patterns of self-hatred (See 23, above). Tattooing. Body modification (self-disfigurement). Conformist behavior re: appearance (fashion) in order to "belong" in groups of people engaged in similar activities.	3, 4
28 Fetishism	foot, etc. A compelling form of addiction—IF the behavior meets all the Five Diagnostic Criteria. Usually considered odd, perverse, even morally deranged, various fetishes, and the syndromes of "acting out" which surround them, often equate fully with the Five Criteria, and are treatable within this context.	1, 2, 3
29 Fantasy	absorption into one's inner life, *at the expense of attending—to the outer world.* The rush of inner torment; negative self-talk, requited or unrequited crushes and secret passions, experiences of consummation, triumph, revenge, failure, shame, loss and/or accomplishment and recognition *(as interior realities within one's fantasy life).*	1, 2, 3

	One's "inner narrative" run amok, by *which one's identity is consumed.* (See 26, above.)	
30 Hoarding, packratting/ clutter	gradual englaciation of living space with "stuff"; inability to let go of things/ possessions. "I just never know when I'm going to kind of need something." A form of constipation in the realm of material possessions. Sentimentality, or the reassurance that "I know it's there when, or if, I (ever) need it." Often a form of incessant security-seeking—powerfully reinforced by that one moment in a thousand when "I" actually do need something I've stashed away—and manage to come up with it!	3, 4
31 Connectivity	need always to be in the nexus of a data stream—or data (generic) streams. Intense anxiety (withdrawal) if disconnected, or cut-off, from constant sources of "input." One relates to the world through screens of "input." An external observer feels he or she is relating, not to a person, but to a human cyborg for whom processing, and responding to, 'data' take precedence over direct human interaction, or connection with "elemental" experiences of nature and the great outdoors. Once "locked in" to the data stream, the person appears very removed from the "here and now'" of the immediate environment. (See 4, above.)	1, 2, 3, 4

32 Virtual reality(ies)	immersion in "synthetic" realities, leading to complete disconnect from "consensus" reality (the one most of us try to live in, most of the time). With the explosive development of the technological capabilities of virtual/synthetic realities, the ability to "compose," construct, "orchestrate" one's absolute, "ideal" escape into an alternative realm of pleasure/pain/romance/power/ domination/submission/sex/fetishes/role-playing/identities, etc. becomes irresistible. One can "actualize" one's innermost fantasies (of whatever description).The orchestration of synthetic realities, however, is, short of bodily death, never finished, for there is always the pursuit of greater "highs" of scenarios (delusional as they are) of "absolute control and acute pleasure/pain" to be added to the "synthetic" mix—especially as the exponentially evolving technology of virtual reality(ies) becomes ever more refined.	1, 2, 3, 4
33 Being a "healer"	"buying one's own trip" as a "healer"—a true, professional "helper," God's "right-hand" man/woman. Taking one's involvement in "healing work" as a validation of oneself as a person. Eventually, with Addiction Energy present, this can lead to a lopsided belief in one's own "healing powers," as if these are a personal possession (making one "especially special"), rather than a gift that is on loan. One becomes inebriated with the "need-to-be-needed" by others, and equally inebriated with being treated as someone (very)	1, 2, 3, 4

special—who possesses such special gifts. Can becoming a "guru" (with anointed followers), complete with a "cult of personality" to match, be far behind?

Note on #33: Buying into one's own trip as a "healer" is one of the most powerful identity intoxicants known to humankind. It is true that people in human services aspire to do "healing work," but we must be careful not to overly identify the "who we are" with the "what we do." Ego inflation, poor boundaries and impaired judgment—and their attendant consequences—are the legacy of such folly. We may do healing work, and we may even be pretty good at it, but we are *not* uniquely talented or gifted as "healers."

Key (Qualities of Indulgence):

1 Central to the experience is the *narrowing focus of attention into a compressed (often visual) space.*
2 Central to the experience is *adrenalin rush—arousal.*
3 Central to experience is *sedation—sedative effects.*
4 Central to the experience is *the illusion of having—or being able to acquire and exert—complete control.*

[Note: the motivations of increasing pleasure, reducing pain, or maintaining the ability to function are givens in all manifestations of Behavioral Addictions, just as with substance-based ones.]

CHAPTER SIX

A First Approach to the Whole Question of Healing

"HEALING" is a loaded word. It can be construed, as an outcome, as meaning anything from a complete cessation and removal of pathological symptoms, on the one hand, to "finding one's way to live" in the ongoing presence of pathological challenges, on the other. Our original list of "qualities" underscores just what a fearsome, multifaceted foe Addiction Energy can be, yet these very qualities have something to contribute to our consideration of just what lines of approach may hold some possibility for actually being helpful. For some of these qualities the hints they hold as to what constitutes healing will seem quite obvious. For other qualities hints about what constitutes healing are more subtle and less obvious.

For this first pass at the whole question of healing, let's now go back over the list of Addiction Energy's qualities, to see what, if anything, each one of them may have, within it, that might be suggestive of possible cures, remedies, or strategic interventions. Perhaps they will suggest measures that can be taken, through which we can influence Addiction Energy in some salutary way.

Note: Whatever we gain from this exercise is likely to be of provisional help only, for the larger question of healing must ultimately take into account the nature of one's very relationship to Addiction Energy in its entirety. This question of what constitutes ultimate possibilities for healing is taken up in Chapter 10.

Here we go, once again, into our "qualities" list:

DISPLACEMENT (A)

The ability of Addiction Energy to manifest in many different areas: both substance- and non-substance-based behaviors.

The hard reality is that, at this point, *there is no known cure that would seem to pertain to this quality of Addiction Energy.* Shunting, or trying to squelch, expression of Addiction Energy to keep it from discharging through any one particular channel only results in its subsequent expression through some other channel, notwithstanding the fact that that subsequent channel may be far-removed and seemingly unrelated to the former outlet through which Addiction Energy was manifesting.

PHYSICAL COMPULSION (B)

An inner itch, body-centered, gravitational attraction—craving.

The cures are more in the form of mitigating remedies that are body-centered, including calming the body down via physical sedation/body-focused meditation; drawing off energy through exercise/exertion; acupuncture, therapeutic massage, yoga; diet (avoiding blood sugar swings/hypoglycemia), staying away from caffeine, refined sugar, along with other foods and toxic substances (as one becomes, over the course of recovery, gradually aware of their deleterious effects)—for even if the ingestion of certain foods and substances does not rise to the level of addiction, their use may further the behaviors that do.

MENTAL OBSESSION (C)

The narrowing of mental focus to a simple, if insistent, strident quest or aim (and all the delusional linkages and distended thought process that go with it).

Here the implied cures are mind-centered, and integrative. They include:

(1) development of insight, integration of the unconscious split-off components of mental functioning (via counseling/psychotherapy, meditation and dream work).

(2) developing another conscious focus/preoccupation (as in work, career, family, self-improvement, hobbies, helping others, etc.).[17]

17. Note: these particular measures feel more like an exercise in "playing for time" rather than cure. Nevertheless, as a measure to, in the moment, head-off the drive to instant gratification via addictive indulgence, developing another conscious focus or preoccupation has its place. These measures, however, should *not* be construed as "positive addictions." This expression gets bandied about from time to time, and is a perversion of the whole concept of Addiction, which, *by definition,* speaks to "increasingly negative consequences over time." Are there "positive" "repetitions," compulsions and obsessions? Arguably, yes (or more likely, "maybe"). Are there "positive addictions?". . . Never.

(3) developing a cosmic, or transpersonal, sensibility in which one's personal struggles and conflicts are recast within the context of a larger conception of reality—a larger whole.

POSSESSION (D)

A quality that is alive, and autonomous, taking on a life of its own, with a different agenda from ego-consciousness.

For this powerful quality, cures are dynamic, and *experience-centered*. They include:

(1) Exorcism (within either a religious or secular context), in which the quality of possession is gotten rid of—eliminated—as "alien," and (therefore) having no rightful claim to be a part of our mix.

(2) *Cessation* of addiction/possession-driven behaviors which, if the cessation is sustained long enough, renders a person a less suitable host for possession energy to occupy. This quality of possession—of being possessed—finally (after a protracted struggle) takes its leave, presumably in search of a more suitable host. This line of approach can be summarized as follows: Behavioral integrity leads to release from Possession—*if* it can be sustained long enough.[18]

---

18. For those you who are inclined to find out a bit more about Possession, including the range of its manifestations along with some prophylactic measures to impede or prevent it's dynamics, a good primer is Chapter 6 ("I Want a Body: Possession Experiences") in the book *You Cannot Die*, by

(3) Finding a spiritual experience to offset the "satanic presence," or "the tyranny of the psychic realm"—"*spiritus contra spiritum.*"[19]

ATTACHMENT (E)

The original "hunger" to exist at all.

For this quality of Addiction Energy, cures, or palliative measures, are primarily philosophical, existential, and spiritual in nature. Borrowing from various traditions (especially Buddhism), we find:

(1) A renunciation of attachments, and their attendant cravings and desires, leads one into an awareness—and an experience—of the essential oneness and interconnectedness and of all living things. A more colloquial way of saying this is that one may discover that: What one seeks through misguided cravings and desires, one already has through "right relations."

Ian Currie. (Note: the full citation for this title is included in the bibliography on page 146.)

19. This brief Latin expression, "*spiritus contra spiritum*" ("spirit" [spiritual agency] against "spirit" [alcohol spirits—'demon rum' et al.]) was the concise formula (for gaining deliverance from active alcoholism) communicated to Bill W. by the Swiss psychiatrist Carl Gustav Jung. It was included in a correspondence from Dr. Jung to Bill W. dated January 30, 1961. The complete correspondence is available online. For Bill W.'s original letter to Dr. Jung, please see http://www.barefootsworld.net/wilsonletter.html. For Dr. Jung's famous reply please see http://www.barefootsworld.net/jungletter.html

(2) the teaching: Love and compassion lead to release from suffering.

(3) the paradoxical peace and acceptance of "being in the world, but not of it," and "being of the world, but not (fully) in it," along with, "wearing the world like a loose garment."

(4) the Al-Anon admonition: "Detach with love."

(5) that part of the recovery path set forth in *Sex and Love Addicts Anonymous* (the basic text for S.L.A.A.) which presents withdrawal as an *elective* experience. One can *choose* a path of active cessation (renunciation) of painful attachment.[20]

(6) the search for a more stable, inner-based personal identity through the process of exploring meditation, yoga and other spiritual disciplines (either formal or self-invented); finding a "center of gravity" of personal identity within oneself, rather than having one's identity held at the mercy (and whim) of external forces, opinions, and other people—of society-at-large.

---

20. For more information on the withdrawal process, including *elective* withdrawal, please consult the S.L.A.A. "Big Book" *(Sex and Love Addicts Anonymous)*, specifically Chapter 5, "The Withdrawal Experience." The full citation for this book is included in the Bibliography on page 146.

"ROUSABLE"/TRIGGERABLE (F)

The ability of Addiction Energy to trigger or rouse—to "show up" anywhere and in any instant—seizing upon any plane of human endeavor.

The implied cures for these strange, imperious qualities have to do with *what* to do with these characteristics of Addiction Energy *when*—rather than if— they show up. In other words, *their bursting upon the scene is to be expected.*

There would appear to be four different kinds of fire-fighting responses:

(1) ***The exorcism*** (either religious or secular) ***model of cure***, in which the energy of triggering/rousability is treated as alien and undesirable, and, therefore, is gotten-rid-of, having no further claims on the individual.

(2) ***The integration model of cure***, in which nothing is disowned as "alien"—all parts of the self are taken in and incorporated. "Splits" and compartmentalizations are eliminated, but ***not*** the energy that comprises them. The energy is accepted, but in a transformed condition/shape—"sublimation."[21]

---

21. It is fascinating to consider four major categories of intrapsychic functioning, especially from the standpoint of what a comprehension of the psychodynamics involved with *each* component has to offer by way of coming to an understanding of the *allocation of psychical energy*. These four categories, "Displacement" (which we've already encountered), "Suppression," "Repression," and "Sublimation" have their roots in late nineteenth- and early twentieth-century psychoanalytic thought. They all pertain aptly to the addiction realm. Here they are:

(1) *Displacement*—an ***un***conscious process by which an energy linked

originally to one part of *past* conscious experience finds discharge through another experience in the present. The "present day" experience may be very far removed from the original experience (seemingly long lost to memory). NOTE: *It requires, consumes, uses up, takes, a considerable amount of energy for energy to be* ***un****consciously redirected or redeployed.*

(2) *Suppression*—a **semi**-conscious process in which whatever it is that one does not want to think about is held, somewhat consciously, away from oneself at (so to speak) "arm's length." This is very common. We all, presumably, have a "to do" list awaiting our attention. Every time we think of something on that list, and quickly say, "I don't want to think about it now; I'll deal with it later"—that is an act of "suppression."
NOTE: *It requires, consumes, uses up, some amount of energy to "suppress" energy (awareness).*

(3) *Repression*—an **un**conscious process in which the energy held regarding something that is *disturbing* to awareness is actively—*though unconsciously*—partitioned off from conscious awareness. From the standpoint of ego-consciousness, whatever the event, or experience that occurred which, if known, would be highly upsetting to the orientation of ego-consciousness, has, *from the standpoint of ego-consciousness, never happened, and (therefore) does not exist.*
NOTE: *It requires and consumes a great deal of energy to repress energy surrounding disturbing events, i.e., to keep unwanted awarenesses out of conscious attention (out of ego-consciousness).*

(4) *Sublimation*—a ***conscious*** *holding of the energy* (and awareness of the experiences that underlie it—to which the energy is linked). Sublimation, in addition to holding awareness of energy and its life-experience-based underpinnings, is also the ongoing act—a kind of consecration—of *consciously* drawing on this energy and the awarenesses it fosters in ways that further "goodness." NOTE: *There is* ***no*** *energy lost or squandered in this process, because nothing is* ***un****conscious about this process.* Nothing is being displaced, suppressed, or repressed. The energy is likely redirected, and the new deployment of the energy is, it is true, an expenditure of this energy, but *this is a conscious, ethical, moral, and perhaps artistic, choice of redirection, rather than an act of avoidance or a manifestation of amnesia.*

(3) *The co-existence model of cure,* which is less a "cure" in the traditional sense, and more an *outcome.* This outcome involves finding a way to come to terms with the fact that Addiction Energy—or at least some significant aspect of it—is a "given" to our life situation. It is structural, having been set in place, "baked in the cake," long before we were conscious enough to have any say over it. As difficult as it may seem to accept this truth, a worthy challenge comes out of it. We are obliged to find a way to accommodate, or co-exist with, the ENERGY, without being destroyed by it. This involves nothing less than mutual toleration, accommodation and/or dialoguing between disparate parts of oneself—pluralistic consciousness accepted—with an attitude of "all parts (of me) have a right to exist."[22] Our personal sense of self, sometimes called our ego-consciousness, is seen as being a part of an "inner family," consisting of (from the standpoint of ego-consciousness) sometimes cooperative, sometimes non-cooperative levels of consciousness and conscious "complexes." This path can lead to befriending one's "inner addict," one's "inner selves," rather than attempting to exorcise them.

---

22. Regarding the discovery that one, in terms of personal identity and ego-consciousness, is a part of an internal "family," or arrangement of "other" awarenessess and consciousnesses, it's important to note that "parts," or aspects (shadow sides) of the human psyche that have been split-off, suppressed and (especially) repressed can, as the energy around them surfaces in the life of a recovering individual, *feel* like forces of alien possession. The longer these "parts," and their energy, have been, in the life history of the person, "underground," the more powerful and alien they may appear to be when they initially surface. However, *these energies are not necessarily alien:* they are, more likely, alien*ated* parts of a more inclusive Self, which includes ego-consciousness along with other split-off consciousnesses.

(4) *The **Self-Pact** model of cure*—This is a new approach which has shown some efficacy with anger and rage addiction, and *that may be more generally applicable across a range of Behavioral Addictions in which the phenomenon of triggering looms large as a precipitating factor in destructive episodes.* The Self-Pact is an *integrative* approach to working with Addiction Energy.[23]

DIS-EASE (G)

The holistic notion that psychological/emotional/spiritual and physical factors which are out of balance with each other lead to sickness at any level.

The implied cure is the restoration of balance of these factors which, when realized, leads to "ease." Dis-ease, in whatever form it takes, is a symptom that, with intention, attempts to draw attention to the existing imbalances that are in need of attention, along with possible remediative or curative factors.

MANIA/MANIACAL (H)

Pressing Urgency: "Self-Justifying"/ Self-Rationalization/ Justification Run Amok.

The implied lines of cure are easily stated, but hard to enact. They include:

---

23. For a thorough presentation of the Self-Pact, please consult my book *Anger and Rage Addiction & The Self-Pact: New Lights on an Old Nemesis* (Four Rivers Press, 2013. fourriverspress.com). See also footnotes 24 & 39 on pages 63 and 124, respectively.

(1) Breaking the system of denial (as to what is really in play with this pressing urgency and rationalization)—in short, establishing some "bedrock honesty" with oneself;

(2) As a result of breaking through to a deeper level of honesty with oneself, experiencing deflation of the ego—of egotistical demands, claims and expectations—*at depth;*

(3) Surrendering to—accepting *at depth*—the reality one is up against;

(4) De-activation, rather than re-activation, meaning relinquishing demands for specific outcomes rather than pressing ahead regardless of consequences, and:

(5) As a result of all of the above, breaking the spell of myopic self-justification and rationalization—"waking up and smelling the coffee" (unless, of course, you're addicted to caffeine!).

DESPERATION (I)

Panicky, reactive, clutching (as in stranglehold), bolting, stampeding.

The implied cures have to do with getting in touch with the emotions and feelings ("affect") present at the time that this desperation-based substrate/foundation of character was being set in place. The following elements of healing may come into play:

(1) The process involved in learning to "digest," "assimilate," come to terms with—or otherwise consciously co-exist with—what can not, in its fundaments, be changed.

(2) Under auspicious circumstances, and always with tremendous, sustained effort, integration—coming into proper resonance with desperation energy—is, to some extent, possible. With a significant realization of this possibility, a life that can be lived "to good purpose, always" can take shape, and hold fast, over the remaining duration of one's lifetime.

(3) This achievement/attainment/realization becomes doable, by increments ("little by slow"), in the life of the recovering person, as earlier—and therefore more deep-seated—manifestations of this still-active quality of Addiction Energy continue to emerge in personal behavior, spurring ever deepening awarenesses.

SEDUCTION/SEDUCTIVE (J)

The quality of being lulled and lured into "trying something"—an indulgence of some sort.

Implied cures are short-term and longer-term:

(1) The implied cure (short term) is to develop "sales resistance" and "street smarts." This can be done by developing some mechanical rules that automatically kick in whenever and wherever a seductive threat presents itself. These rules, once enacted, short-circuit a vulnerable, or susceptible, thought

process, and quickly get a person clear of harm—out of harm's reach.

(2) The larger picture (longer-term): Observing—becoming a student of—one's own areas of susceptibility—of areas in which one can (still) be seduced. This is tantamount to initiating a practice of *mindfulness*, which involves learning to observe the rising and falling of one's own cycles of desire: feeling the feelings (as they come and go, rise and fall) *without acting (out) on them.*

OPPORTUNISTIC/OPPORTUNISM (K)

Constant scanning for weakness and vulnerability.

The implied cure for this quality is to develop a keen, sustained mindfulness of one's personal vulnerability, keying on the fact that *both* the vulnerability, *and* the mindfulness to come to terms with it, remain components of living, day in and day out, *no matter how "cured" a person may feel or experience themself to be.* The distinction between "living in reprieve," and being "cured," is held, at all times, as a focus of awareness. The adage, "'Reprieve,' when it has gone on for a long time, may come to feel like 'cure,' but IT NEVER IS," remains emblazoned in awareness.

Note: one feature of this cure is that when we encounter temptation—or are ambushed by it—it plays to what is expected, rather than being taken as evidence of a person's being a failure, or "not working my program hard enough," or otherwise screwing up or doing something wrong.

SELF-LOATHING/SELF-HATRED (L)

Felt about oneself, but often projected outwards onto the external world.

The implied cure is to develop the capacity—the "inner muscle"—to stand fast—stay put—under the assault of this kind of self-trashing energy, and to learn to "ride the energy" *inwards*. In so doing one is put in touch with its origins—the original causes and conditions that have led to self-condemnation and self-destructive expression. Getting in touch with primary causes and conditions helps to neutralize the negative expression of this energy, freeing it up to be drawn upon in more constructive ways.[24]

24. This paragraph on "cure" for the energy of self-hatred is a highly abbreviated setting forth of what is central to a new approach called the Self-Pact. This approach has already proven useful in dealing with the dynamics of "triggering" phenomena so endemic to anger and rage addiction. It is thoroughly presented in *Anger and Rage Addiction & The Self-Pact; New Lights on an Old Nemesis* (Four Rivers Press, 2013. fourriverspress.com). The Self-Pact has considerable potential to address, and help, afflicted individuals work their way out of the maelstrom of destructiveness characterized by the phenomenon of "triggering." Triggering, as a phenomenon, occurs across a range of addictions. As of this writing, the possible fuller utility of the Self-Pact for addictions which, in addition to anger and rage addiction, have triggering as a significant part of their dynamic, has yet to be further explored.

THE NEGATIVE RUSH (M)

Getting high on destructiveness.

The implied cure is the re-introduction (or rediscovery) of personal conscience—of finding something in the outer world, or within oneself, that "truly matters." Leaving a legacy of rage, destructiveness, self-hatred, bloodlust, sadism, cruelty, tragedy and loss, all at-the-ready to infect the next unsuspecting generation, becomes deeply felt as pathetic and undesirable. Finding a path that can offset the past's cascading juggernaut of acid-laced outworkings and their toxic consequences becomes desired at depth. As described in the previous section on the energy of self-hatred, the energy of triggering into rageful acts can be harnessed and "ridden inwards," leading to essential life-changing experiences and realizations.

METASTASIS (N)

The all-consuming/all-expressing collective manifestations of Addiction Energy—the ENERGY!!—which has been "spreading" (metastasizing), undiagnosed and untreated, for a considerable length of time.

The implied avenue for healing (if healing in late-stage metastatic addiction is even possible) is a massive assault on the entire symptomatology—the outflow channels through with Addiction Energy is issuing. Metaphorically, this is the equivalent of combined radiation and chemotherapy for metastasized cancers. Only a "full frontal assault" in a contained environment in which the interlocking, negatively synergistic spillways—

both substance-based and non-substance-based—can be wrestled with all of a piece, has any chance of providing the necessary impact. As untreated addiction is lethal, late-stage intervention with metastatic addiction requires extensive and "heroic" measures, if it is to stand any chance of being at all successful.

VITALITY/"ELAN VITAL" (O)

The motive force behind all manifestation.

The notion of 'cure' for this underlying quality—and source—of Addiction Energy is a bit miscast, for here we are not talking about healing something that is "sick"—but, rather, an outcome of incorporating something that is intrinsic, basic, and *healthy*. The premise for this outcome is that once the pathological outworkings of Addiction Energy are reconnoitered, consciously engaged, and reconciled, what remains is . . . *ENERGY*. This *ENERGY* is the very energy of creation and life itself. In its unpolluted state, it is a pure resource to be drawn upon for the benefit of all levels: mind, body, spirit and heart.

The reclaiming of the *ENERGY* that has, through addiction, been co-opted and distended into self-destructive manifestation is likely a life-long task, arrived at only very gradually. To the extent that this outcome takes form, it is attained through a long process of coming into proper alignment with, coming into proper resonance with—"taming," after a fashion, this basic vitality—and then drawing on this reclaimed reservoir to be "energized!": to animate one's life in any area of endeavor.

In short, "energy for living" means having the resources to encounter, ever more richly, the reality that is before one, thereby increasing one's capacity for a wider experience of emotional, mental, physical, and spiritual life, including relating, creating, and being of service to others.

NOTE re: The ENERGY OF VITALITY

Although theoretically possible, the challenge of coming into proper alignment with, coming into proper resonance with—the taming and claiming Addiction Energy in service of healthy living—is very, very difficult and fraught with risk. If successful, the dividends are immense. They are the fruits of a profoundly redeemed life. Within the professional field of addictions counseling, it is unclear whether this standard should ever be a specified treatment goal. It should certainly not ever be set forth as a specific treatment goal in the early going of any recovering addict. The possibility of such a profound outcome may become a product of the life-odyssey of recovery, unfolding, as it may or will, over the course of decades.

NOTE re: Practical Options for Healing

In summary, drawing on all the territory we have covered thus far, healing involves three basic possibilities:

(1) *Exorcism: subtypes—*
Religious, as in the "casting out of devils."
Secular, as in "character defect removal," the getting rid of "what doesn't belong."

(2) *Co-existence* with Addiction Energy—
Living to good purpose, regardless of the ongoing presence of this still destructive potential.

(3) *Integration with the Energy—*
Coming into proper alignment with; coming into proper resonance with, Addiction Energy, in which, with addiction "tamed" and "claimed," the Energy—*ENERGY*—remains as a reservoir of vitality with which the recovering person is engaged in a deepening, mutual correspondence and shared, ongoing experience.

NOTE: Here is the meta-question:

As we heal from the negative outworkings of Addiction Energy, is the Energy of Addiction—the *ENERGY!!*—also healed: fundamentally transformed in some positive way?[25]

25. The question of what the ultimate nature of one's relationship is with Addiction Energy, with further attention to healing possibilities, is taken up in Chapter 10.

CHAPTER SEVEN

The Sequencing of Behavioral and Substance-based Addictions

WE HAVE PAID QUITE A BIT of attention to providing a sound basis for bridging the conceptual gap between drug addiction/alcoholism and Behavioral Addictions, based on the Five Diagnostic Criteria derived from the alcohol/drug addiction universe. As a result we have had to conclude that Addiction is, first and foremost, an outworking of an *ENERGY!!* (Addiction Energy). Then, having taken a closer look at the qualities and characteristics of this energy, parsed through a number of specific behavioral addictions, and finally (phew!) gone over the list of characteristics of Addiction Energy once more, (this time with an eye to discerning what, if anything, each characteristic might contribute to gaining some comprehension of a healing possibility, potential or line of approach for this energy), we must now address the question of sequence.

Here it is in a nutshell: Behavioral Addictions may *precede, coincide with,* or *develop subsequent to* substance-based addictions. Additionally, there are, as well, many people who have full-blown Behavioral Addictions who have never used, nor will ever use, a chemical compound, including alcohol, as a part of their pattern of addictive behaviors.

What follows is a presentation of three sketches, or vignettes, that exemplify how Behavioral Addictions can launch in each of the three instances. Bear in mind, however, that the case material I am going to present, although compelling, is suggestive only. There are so many variations on a theme as to how Behavioral Addictions can arise, and manifest, that the examples offered will be woefully incomplete in covering such a wide swath of territory. Nevertheless, in presenting these vignettes, the *resonance* of the process through which these afflictions come to be is clearly visible—and feel-able—and this *resonance* of origins, sequence and outworkings *does* seem to apply universally. These case vignettes should be helpful in furthering understanding of the provenance of Behavioral Addictions in many other areas, as they can arise, be lived out, and, ultimately, be identified and treated.[26]

Let's start with an example of Behavioral Addiction *preceding* the development of substance-based addictions.

The family of origin of this person was (self-report) described as "war-torn," violent, addiction-ridden, a "toxic-waste-dump." His father was alcoholic and abusive. His mother was a classic

---

26. These case vignettes are the reported experiences of two men and one woman. Considering that the overall developmental dynamics of Behavioral Addictions as they may precede, coincide with, and/or follow active alcoholism and drug addiction are very similar for women and men, each of the experiences reported here could just as easily be those of a person of the other gender, including from among the ranks of those who experience themselves as transgender.

enabler, trying, sometimes nobly, to "do the right thing," although, when the chips were down, she put appeasing her alcoholic husband ahead of actively intervening to protect the wellbeing of her children.

This man described his take-away from his childhood background as "residual, and triggerable, feelings of terror and desperation." His early survival strategy involved a determination to be exceptional—how to "feel good" became the quest, and, in hindsight, these strivings were really attempts at finding a way how NOT to feel the emotions from the past—past trauma. As he stated many years later, "Many people are concerned with whether there is life after death. I was concerned with finding out whether or not there was life after birth."

This man had a precocious musical talent leading to "applause moments" in elementary school when he would play his instrument at school assemblies. These applause moments were transcendent experiences for him—moments of being the object of communal "love" and adoration. They were "moments of being truly alive"—moments during which, ephemeral as the were, no trauma history was sensed, and there was truly, at least for a moment, "life after birth."

As a freshman at an inner city high school, where, if you were a freshman, you were "the lowest form of life," subject to frequent hazing and bullying, he won a leading role in the freshman class play. At this school, each class year worked up its own play, and all four class years presented them on one Friday evening in late October. As our person relates, "I was only a freshman and had been at this school only six weeks—I was terrified of being bullied—of being 'hit on' like that every day I went there—and then, suddenly, three thousand kids knew me by my first name!" Hazing stopped. Bullying was greatly reduced and he had his first experience with the acquisition of a kind of power, influence, and security that arose, once again, from being "exceptional."

It was about the same time that this individual discovered active, intentional sexual experience. He reported that with parental guidance at home being so lacking, the subject of sexuality was labeled (in loud tones) as "vulgar," and peremptorily dismissed as a forbidden topic. So, this person's discovery of orgasmic experience was acquired through "street knowledge"—being taught how to masturbate by his peers. The accompanying discovery of the transporting power of the orgasm ushered in, with immediacy, a pattern of compulsive masturbation. "I thought I had stumbled upon some secret power that really rules the world, but which seems to be largely taboo, unacknowledged and disregarded in the everyday world," he said.

In his mid-teens, not long after having discovered the transforming power of the orgasm, he discovered the "cure by (falling in) love." The experience of falling in love was unanticipated, therefore by ambush. He had walled himself off so thoroughly by shutting down uncomfortable emotions of any sort that he had steeled himself against letting in any surprising encounter of an emotional nature. When the walls were breached, the experience of falling in love was transporting. It was, for this person, the emotional equivalent of physical orgasm—the experience of losing ego boundaries—the dissolving of the sense of where "I" end and where "you" begin, as these boundaries expand, enmesh and merge with one another.

The love affair that resulted, as enthralling as it was, did not take precedence over compulsive masturbation and the outer world experiments with "chasing the orgasm" involving additional third-parties. Being "in love," emotionally needy and therefore "committed," went head-to-head with the chase after wanton sexual oblivion wherever, in the outer world, it could be found. But, as this person reported, "I was more committed to, and more dependent on, this person [the primary, romantic partner] than I realized. Once I had fallen in love, I was split. Emotional security I had to have at all costs, but sexual oblivion would constantly lure me on, and I would go . . . In hindsight, I realize that I had two decidedly split neurological arrangements taking turns in my body. One was the 'committed' person, taking the presence and constancy of my partner thoroughly for granted; the other was the constant imperious quest for self-oblivion through sexual encounter and emotional intensity with anyone I could find. I was a house divided."

The first love affair ended for this person at about the two-year point, when he was in his late teens. "I had no idea how dependent I had become on this partner as my 'second set of lungs,'" he said. "I took this person's presence in my life completely as a given. I was to learn that if you want to discover the size of a bomb after it has detonated, you can gauge it by measuring the dimensions of the crater it leaves behind." When his partner broke up with him—when the bomb of unanticipated rupture and loss went off—this person hurtled, unexpectedly (again by ambush) into the withdrawal experience from the break-up of this first love affair. As part of the withdrawal experience, he felt suicidal and began to engage in daredevil, risk-taking behaviors. He reported, for example, having placed a .22 caliber Lugar semi-automatic pistol to his temple, while standing on the sloped roof of a house, and then, with index finger on the trigger, experimenting with "trigger pressure" on the revolver while the gun was so directed.

It was against this immediate backdrop of a blown-up love affair, while reeling from the symptoms of withdrawal from this love-affair break-up combined with a growing indulgence in dare-devil/risk-taking behaviors, that he discovered the transforming power of alcohol. Alcohol and other substance-based addictions were launched as a direct result of his need to manage withdrawal symptoms from Behavioral Addictions ("love" addiction—attachment hunger/morbid dependency; sex addiction—compulsive attempts to rearrange his internal reality through oblivion via orgasm; and risk/dare-devil behaviors—burying powerful emotions under the onslaught of adrenalin rushes stemming from arousal seeking, thrill seeking, sensation-seeking, and intensity-seeking behaviors).

An alcoholic and drug addict was born of this mix, but, as should be clear from this example, Addiction Energy—in the form of the desperation to survive—that drive to find a way to deny the misery of his turbulent world, as aided by escaping the world altogether via immersion into self-annihilating indulgences ("applause" moments, dare-devil/risk behaviors, arousal seeking, thrill-seeking, sensation-seeking, intensity-seeking, adrenalin-junkie behaviors)—all this was operative in this person's life very early in the game. *Alcoholism and substance-based addictions are, in this example, relatively late arrivals on the scene.*

Here is our second example. This is a very brief sketch of a person in whom Behavioral Addiction develops *alongside* a concurrent substance-based addiction.

The starting point for this case vignette is a person in his late teens who commenced and then came to rely on "recreational use" of alcohol and/or drugs, and whose usage finally crossed the line into addiction. In other words, the Five Diagnostic Criteria of addiction have taken root. For this person, inhibition-lowering experiences with alcohol and other chemical compounds led to further exploration of avenues of pleasure or instant gratification. Combining substances (crystal meth, cocaine, "bath salts," or any of the "flavor of the moment" plethora of new designer molecules that inundate "the street" almost daily), along with arousal-seeking activities (as in "partying," sexual promiscuity, thrill-seeking, "naughty" or forbidden, even illicit, behaviors to heighten the overall intensity of addiction experiences) became the norm.

This person, as time went on, increasingly withheld himself from real social interactions. He became something of a pariah or outcast due to social misbehavior, including some instances of more progressed antisocial behavior. With his reputation tarnished, he took refuge in more solitary, sedating or numbing activities, such as internet-based pornography, chat rooms and videogames—in which his "world" (as viewed by an external observer) would become smaller—condensed into the dimensions of a video screen, and therefore seemingly more manageable.

This person placed utmost importance on maintaining the illusion of being effective, functional—of being in control. *His* experience of the "video-screen world" was that *it* became larger, eventually coming to encompass, and then become, his "world." As this immersion into the solitary realm continued, the person later reported, "I was more and more in control of less and less, until I was in complete control of nothing."

Reporting on the further progression of this pattern in this person is beyond the scope of the immediate task at hand, which is to demonstrate how Behavioral Addictions can arise concurrent with drinking and drugging. That part has been shown. Suffice it to say that from this point forward, this person was increasingly consumed by *both* substance-based and Behavioral Addictions. In this particular case, it was the substance-based addiction that, eventually, forced him to seek help. It remained for this person, once "clean and sober," to encounter the painful reality, and the awakening of awareness of that reality, that Behavioral Addictions were still roiling the waters, and, in the fullness of time, needed also to be addressed. This situation of a person, once "clean and sober" (in terms of drug addiction and alcoholism), awakening to the presence of Behavioral Addiction, is focused on more specifically in the next case example.

Once again, I wish to emphasize that there are many avenues for the co-development of substance-based and Behavioral Addictions. The "amplification factor"—the ramping up of intensity of addiction indulgences by combining non-substance-based and substance-based activities becomes a common launching element in many of them.

One variation on this theme is when a behavioral indulgence is resorted to as a way to try to counterbalance the negative effects of drinking and drugging, or vice versa. This strategy of pitting one form of indulgence against another in an attempt to control either one makes the "new arrival," whether substance-based or purely behavioral, seem like a virtuous attempt at "self-management."[27] This delusion leads soon enough to the mutual reinforcement of intensity—a true negative synergy—that is a hallmark of all such "hybrid" addictions.

Our third example is a case vignette which demonstrates something of how Behavioral Addictions can develop even after recovery from active alcoholism and drug addiction has begun. These are Behavioral Addictions that develop in the course of early recovery, meaning the person in recovery has already made a commitment to become involved in self-help groups and is regularly attending meetings, and has established a foothold in being sober (in terms of alcohol), and abstinence (in terms of drugs) on a daily basis.

The starting point for this example is a person in their early thirties who is in early sobriety, having lived out a pattern of active alcoholism and drug addiction for about ten years. She has joined A.A. and N.A. and goes to meetings regularly.

This person reported, "In my early sobriety/abstinence I truly believed, in the absence of much additional self-knowledge, that all my apparent problems were attributable to my years of active alcoholism and drug addiction. In fact, one of

27. One of many truisms about addiction is: "If you're looking for control, you've lost it."

the early 'messages' that reached me when I started to attend A.A. meetings was the 'all-you-have-to-do-is-stop-drinking/stop-using—get sober and clean—and-everything-will-be-wonderful' kind of logic. I guess I was a bit of a sucker to go for the 'instant gratification' appeal of this message. In hindsight, I realize that this message is consistent with what is sometimes called the 'pink cloud stage' of early recovery."

Her narrative continues: "I was going to a meeting a day—mostly A.A., but sometimes N.A., joined and got active in a group, had gotten myself a sponsor and was starting to take a look at the Twelve Steps. I was working hard on my sobriety, trying to shore up the damaged relationship with my partner; I decided to try to lose some weight, took up jogging and some rigorous exercise, even quit smoking! Life was good."

She later reported that, in hindsight, she came to realize that this "rush into health" consisted of virtue-based attempts to become "the person I always thought I should be." "I was attempting to impose on myself perfect adherence to moral and ethical standards. That's what I thought recovery was."

Over a number of months (this person was sober about 15 months at this point) she reported having "a growing awareness that I'm doing some of the 'getting well' things on my recovery 'to do' list in a way that is starting to feeling compulsive to me. It's not so much that I'm enjoying doing them. I'm just kind of concerned about how I'll feel if I STOP doing them. From time to time, I would even wonder if I might be addicted to them, but I wasn't at all sure about this. Was I becoming 'addicted?' . . . or were they simply normative societal behaviors that 'everybody' engages in?"

Before proceeding further with this story, let's recap where we are with it thus far: So far we've been hearing about someone who gets clean and sober and goes to A.A. meetings and N.A. meetings regularly, has a sponsor, gets active with a group, condenses all her problems (and hopes) into the "All-I-have-to-do-is-not-drink/drug-and-everything-will-be-wonderful-or-at-least-get-better," one-size-fits-all, "pink cloud" illusion, who throws herself at recovery, charging headlong into 'self-improvement'—eliminating obvious "bad habits" (like smoking) and embarking on healthy activities like exercise regimens and diets and weight-loss, and who has some growing sense that a lot of what she is up to is really quite compulsive, and maybe even begins to seriously question whether there may be addiction overtones to some of what's going on.

Here's where things took a decided turn:

A behavioral pattern started to be felt that seemed to have "taken on a life of its own"—in this case, it was reported first in the area of compulsive overeating, as evidenced by weight gain (after the dieting bit the dust). This person subsequently reported starting to be beset with obsessional intrigues about potential (at least in fantasy) romantic and sexual partners outside her marriage. Also, this person reported spending more and more time online, checking out social media chat sites, and getting deeply immersed in a few longstanding hobbies (in her case, gardening and sky-diving). Despite her commitment to "recovery" along with maintaining regular attendance at meetings, these extra-recovery activities were increasingly becoming "worlds unto themselves," more and more displacing this person from being consistently present in the everyday world of duties, obligations, and responsibilities—including tending to her "recovery."

This behavioral pattern eventually led to an episode of "acting out"—NOT relapse in the alcoholism/drug addiction realm, but, rather, a behavioral transgression that was clearly out of the mainstream of what was acceptable—*as gauged by the "sober and recovering"* (in terms of alcohol and substances) *person herself.* In other words, this person's behavior had transgressed one of her innermost values, and *this person* ***noticed it.***[28]

In the case of this person, despite her self-awareness of the transgression, this problematic behavior pattern continued. To keep it going the person's acting out of Behavioral Addictions was "driven underground," and this person, from this point on until the whole charade collapsed several years later, was taken up with living, and managing, an increasingly closed, divided, compartmentalized existence, with one foot in the land of "recovery" and respectability, and the other foot in a parallel world of active addiction and hidden, off-scene behaviors.

---

28. It is not necessary to mention the specific misdoing this person engaged in. In any sample of people in early recovery, behaviors that could cause moral and ethical grief are numerous. The common thread here is that such a behavior, *whatever* it may be, is a violation of an inwardly held moral and ethical code (however personal, private and idiosyncratic this may be) which results in enough personal turmoil to bring a person to awareness either that (1) s/he has violated his or her own code of inner values, or (2) that s/he even *possesses* such a code—something of which s/he may not have been aware until this code was unwittingly violated. Stated more prosaically, this happenstance can be considered to be the re-awakening of conscience.

This concludes the vignette proper. This little case history demonstrates how a Behavioral Addiction—and a *pattern* of Behavioral Addictions—can arise in the life of someone who is recovering, and committed to recovering, from alcoholism and drug addiction, and, without conscious volition or intent, finds themself in the soup once again.

If you're interested in how stories like this can resolve, I offer the following perspectives. These perspectives are no longer the recounting of a single case, but rather, an extract from the healing odyssey of many cases of this sort.

If a person is, relative to their alcoholism/substance-based addictions, involved with A.A./N.A., etc., and is also endeavoring to work the Twelve Steps of recovery, an extreme, discordant behavioral episode—an "outlying" one that brings the whole addictive syndrome involving this behavior to awareness—may show up as a part of a Step Four inventory list, and, sooner or later, be shared (disclosed) to another person (sponsor, counselor, or trusted "other") as part of Step Five. The act of disclosure to a third party of such a behavior and its addictive resonance is often resisted out of a fear that "If I dare name it, it will become *real.*"

On the other hand, if it is disclosed, there is often the naïve assumption—wishful thinking, really, that if "I" name something—admit to something—that is problematic about myself, then just making the admission (which unto itself can demand a lot of courage) will be tantamount to the difficulty's being removed. However . . . and here is the rub . . . there is the discovery that all "naming" and "admitting"—having put the problem on record—have done is to have made the problem a *conscious* one, but . . . *the specific behavior, in all its addictive trappings, is still there and still operative and ongoing.* The problem behavior is *still happening!*

As a former client who was sober in A.A. about 14 months and had just disgorged the fact that he, having gotten married eight months into sobriety and found himself, within two months of the wedding, falling "head-over-heels 'in love'" with an A.A. newcomer, once said to me: "I realized as I shared my fifth step with my sponsor that the very activity I was admitting to, although it was driving me crazy—and despite my getting a migraine headache during the process of taking the Fifth Step—that on that very day I knew I would be 'back at it' again before the clock struck midnight . . . and I was."

It is also possible, of course, that what has happened in the lives of so many people who appear to develop a new Behavioral Addiction in their alcoholism/substance-based addiction recoveries is not so much that the form of addiction is new, per se, but, rather, that there has been the development, in these people, of a new consciousness or awareness. *That* new consciousness, in the absence of being thwarted by re-submergence in substance-based intoxication, has become capable of grasping the existence of an addictive behavioral pattern that may already have been of longstanding. The capacity to become conscious and aware of new areas of addictive acting-out in the lives of nominally sober and clean alcoholics and drug addicts—*that* capacity, in which "problem areas" in recovery make their way onto a Step Four inventory list; get shared with a another person in the context of the Fifth Step; then turn out to be addictions unto themselves; and then, ultimately, get dealt with through living one's way through Steps Six and Step Seven—is actually a triumph of the evolution of recovery. This profound right of passage is, short of being aborted by re-submergence in active alcoholism and drug addiction, an inevitable milestone of growth in the larger tapestry of one's recovery. The formula is: What may start as a suspicion of the existence of a specific Behavioral Addiction and gets listed on a Fourth Step inventory, often becomes, by the time a person "is entirely ready" to undergo the "Step Six" experience of having to "surrender" it, *its own "Step One" experience in terms of that specific behavior.* In other words, the Behavioral Addiction that gets listed on an A.A. "Step four" inventory, eventually becomes a "First Step" admission of personal powerlessness and life-unmanageability—on its *own* inventory.

Another way of looking at this is that what starts, in the recovery process from alcoholism and drug addiction, as an admission that "I am powerless over alcohol and drugs" and the subsequent "surrender" to that reality, leads, over time, to additional 2nd . . . 3rd . . . 4th . . . nth . . . surrenders that become necessary as areas in which Addiction Energy is still operative are discovered. This often drawn-out process leads, gradually yet insistently, to the "becoming entirely ready" line-up of mind, soul, body, spirit and heart which makes yet another surrender possible. In the aggregate, what starts as a "surrender" regarding alcohol and drugs as an alcoholic or drug addict becomes, in the fullness of an enlarged body of experience, personal growth and awareness, a surrender to life—to life on life's terms—as a human being.

CHAPTER EIGHT

Perspectives on Diagnosing and Treating Behavioral Addictions In Oneself, and In Others

O.K. It's time to reiterate a declaration. This book is written both for all those who are wondering about Behavioral Addictions, specifically whether or not they "have them," *and* also for all those who are practitioners in the field of addictions treatment, and who may, in addition to wondering about the status of their clients, be wondering if they, though treatment professionals themselves, also "have them."

There is a deep-rooted tradition within the addictions treatment field that *the most important diagnosis is a self-diagnosis.* This acknowledgment stems from the fact that the professionalized field of addictions treatment owes its existence, by and large, to those who successfully traveled the mutual-help route (A.A., N.A.) to recovery, in the absence of any kind of organized professional field. They had the courage to see themselves, and diagnose themselves, in a vacuum of any reliable, informed professional guidance. They dared to diagnose themselves . . . and they were correct in their diagnosis and the treatment regimen that they developed to treat it! We owe them.

Therefore, consistent with this book's primary purpose, this chapter on diagnosis and treatment has two sections: the first is devoted to all those who are wondering—or more likely, ruminating—about themselves and whether they "do" or whether they "don't" (have a Behavioral Addiction), and a second section in which the presentation is more "professional," tailored to those working in the field who need some professional guidelines that may pertain to their clients (as well as, perhaps, to themselves).

Perspectives on Self-Diagnosing and Self-Treating Behavioral Addictions

For those of you approaching this topic as an outgrowth of your own recovery from alcoholism and drug addiction, your wondering about the existence of other addictions in your life has likely surfaced as a result of some experiences in recovery that have gotten your attention, and, quite possibly, been upsetting or even dismaying to you.

This I say to you right at the outset: you have a lot of company. More people than you can possibly fathom are, in their recoveries, caught up in this kind of serious pondering. Tremendous emphasis is placed, within self-help fellowships like A.A. and N.A., on "character defect removal," the thrust of which is the concern of Steps 6 and 7 (especially as presented in A.A.'s book *Twelve Steps and Twelve Traditions*). Yet the expression "character defects" is really a kind of euphemism that renders the extent of a person's bedevilments less threatening, and therefore more approachable. In fact, the sum and substance of self-diagnosis is originally enshrined in the Step 4 chapter of the *Twelve & Twelve,* in which the labels for whatever afflictions are negatively impacting a person's recovery are left up to the person themself to decide. A number of euphemisms, by way of example, are offered in this regard, including the aforementioned "defects of character"[29] ("character defects"), the "Seven Deadly Sins" (pride, lust, envy, greed, anger, gluttony and sloth), "index of maladjustments" (my personal favorite), "violations of moral principles," "instincts in collision," "physical and mental liabilities," "emotional deformities," "instinct run wild," "instincts on rampage," and so on.

Some of these euphemistic expressions make the problems to be dealt with seem like little pesky gusts of wind, for which certain adjustments, or minor tweaks, of character will provide the solution. Other expressions on this list, such as " . . . Deadly Sins," "instinct run wild" and "instincts on rampage . . . " point, or at least hint, at something far deeper and more sinister.

Most significant, however, is this: The *essence* of that part of the Fourth Step chapter in the *Twelve & Twelve* that introduces such terms and expressions as labels for what may be bedeviling a recovering person is to *give permission for a recovering person to decide for themself, on an individual basis, which labels or expressions feel most right* by way of *self*-diagnosing

29. The expression "defects of character" received original mention in A.A.'s "Big Book" *Alcoholics Anonymous* (1939), and was included, and added to, fourteen years later, in *Twelve Steps and Twelve Traditions* (1953).

whatever it is that is raising havoc—regardless of whether a person seizes upon one of the examples given as self-description, *or chooses to coin his or her own label, topic heading or expression because it feels more "correct," "accurate," or "useful."* The ultimate comment here is: "Having found the shoes that fit, he ought to step into them and walk with new confidence that he is at last on the right track."[30] [31] [32]

Back to the question of diagnosing whether or not you have a Behavioral Addiction right alongside your recovery: If

---

30. *Twelve Steps and Twelve Traditions*, "Step Four" chapter, page 48.

31. A closing note on this point: One hears a great deal, both in recovery and professional circles, about the diagnostic criteria for a whole range of supposed human afflictions as set forth in the "DSM" *(Diagnostic and Statistical Manual of Mental Disorders).* The truth is, the various editions of the DSM bear out the fact that diagnoses come in and go out of fashion, and they are often linked to advocacy groups—especially pharmaceutical companies and those who are subsidized by them—who lobby for the recognition of various syndromes and the inclusion of certain diagnoses. There is money—potentially huge profits—involved with all this. Although some addiction-related diagnoses starting to appear in DSM-V (the current edition of the DSM) may appear useful or applicable, DSM-V (like the DSMs that preceded it) is woefully behind the times in recognizing in some helpful, non-subsidized way the "street reality" when it comes to the state of addictions diagnosis and treatment. All of this is simply to say: Don't be cowed by the DSM. Its process is seriously flawed and contentious, and morally and ethically questionable. As set forth in the Fourth Step chapter of the *Twelve & Twelve,* come up with your own self-diagnostic categories if none of the prevailing ones seem to fit, and . . . "Having found the shoes that fit, . . . step into them and walk with new confidence that" YOU "are at last on the right track."

32. For those of you who have an interest in learning about the rough-and-tumble history of the DSMs, I encourage you to read the article "Nosologies: the future of an illusion," (Times Literary Supplement [TLS] May 18, 2012 issue).

it is an addiction, we are likely not speaking here of a simple "character defect" such as tardiness or "occasionally getting cross" with one's spouse. Addictions, overall, are not "troublesome gusts of wind" (although episodically they may occasionally seem like this). They become, rather (to maintain the metaphor), "hurricanes laced with tornadoes." It is of more than passing interest that in "Step Seven" Chapter of the *Twelve &Twelve,* in which the rigors of what it really takes to face, headlong, destructive behavior, and cease it, are set forth, the author (Bill W., A.A.'s co-founder) lets his hair down a bit. In lieu of the less intimidating and more user-friendly "defects of character" label, he uses the expressions, "overwhelming compulsions and desires, " and "devastating handicaps."

It is in these more extreme manifestations of destructive behavior—provided that, in YOUR judgment, they meet the Five Diagnostic Criteria present in all addictions (as set forth on pp. 13–14)—that it may be apropos, correct, useful and helpful for you to make a diagnosis of a Behavioral Addiction for yourself. The hardest part is getting to the point of recognition. No one likes undergoing "what it takes" to be ready to "see it," let alone "do something about it." But, the good news is, once the Five Diagnostic Criteria of addiction are recognized (assuming they are all there), the path ahead becomes, if not exactly easier, at least more recognizable and doable. You will have demystified what's going on, and what you're up against. Also, you've been there before with alcoholism and/or drug addiction, so, after a fashion, you know what's next. As previously menioned, what likely found its way onto a Fourth Step inventory list within A.A. or N.A., *has now become its own Step One*—complete with powerlessness and the need for surrender—in the immediate area of concern.

If you choose to reveal that you are wrestling with "xyz" Behavioral Addiction at your local A.A. or N.A. meetings, don't expect the resident culture of your local A.A. or N.A. groups to automatically embrace you with support or even understanding and compassion. You may well encounter a degree of intolerance or hostility from those who are similarly afflicted, but, as yet, may be clueless about it. Personal defensiveness, in the form or "taking offense" is a normal reaction for those who may "have it," but aren't anywhere near ready to "see it." They may even cast your sharing as a threat to the Fifth Tradition—the need to keep the meeting focused on its "primary purpose" (carrying the "message" to the alcoholic or addict). (This Tradition need not be so narrowly construed, however.) If you press ahead with some disclosure of your deeply personal and troublesome problems as they relate to your experience of the diversely manifesting energy of addiction, the risk of being censured by those who are threatened by what they aren't ready, or able, to see in themselves will likely be offset by the responses from others at the meeting in whom your disclosures meet with identification and *resonance*. The fact of the entwinement of Behavioral Addictions with both "active" and "inactive" alcoholism and drug addiction makes their presence inseparably integral to almost all stories of substance-based addiction. In truth, in the current era a "pure" history of "only" alcoholism or drug addiction is rarely, if ever, to be found. Therefore, *someone* in an A.A. or N.A. meeting is likely to identify with what it is you choose to reveal. If you can survive the possible rough-and-tumble of initial disclosures, and make connection with other alcoholics and drug addicts who are in recovery and for whom your disclosures ring true, you're on your way to finding fellowship and mutual support. These are of inestimable value in coming to terms with any addiction.

It may turn out that seeking out a Twelve-Step-oriented fellowship that addresses "primary purpose" issues which, at the outset, are closer to what you're now dealing with could be a much better idea than figuring that "I can deal with it all in A.A./N.A." If such a fellowship exists, be prepared to travel considerable distances to get to meetings. The relative inconvenience of having to do this is fully offset by the communal acceptance and identification that comes with finding, relative to the specific Behavioral Addiction one is dealing with, one's "tribe," and accessing the loving support, immediate acceptance, understanding and sharing of "experience, strength and hope"—all priceless assets of fellowship—that await you there.

If no such self-help Twelve-Step-oriented fellowship exists in your area of concern, and you have a lot of courage—although desperation will also do—*you can start one.* At meetings of A.A./N.A., with your newly refined sensitivity to the very issues (Behavioral Addictions) you are now aware of and dealing with within yourself, without necessarily initiating your own personal disclosures, start listening for the "music behind the words" that others in recovery, from time to time, are disclosing regarding their own recoveries and the challenges they are encountering. Sooner or later you'll hear someone share who will be talking about exactly what you have been wrestling with. This person may not yet have the "Behavioral Addictions" awareness that you now have, but the dynamics underlying what that person is sharing will be unmistakable to you. You can trust this resonance you're feeling from what you've heard this person say, and the ground is likely open to your making an approach to this person to explore "shared territory." Humble beginnings for a new Twelve-Step-oriented fellowship addressing a specific Behavioral Addiction? Yes . . . but *that is how they all start.* And, once you have experienced the healing potential that arises with personal experience and vulnerability being mutually shared with another, your own recovery will strengthen, and you'll be on your way.[33]

If you're already in counseling or psychotherapy, your recognition of your own Behavioral Addiction, and your introducing that topic into your counseling and psychotherapy sessions will likely liven up these sessions considerably. The energy that comes to the surface through these discussions can be felt as an affirmation of the timeliness and rightness of "being on the right track."[34]

---

33. A highly useful resource for those of you who may find yourselves undertaking the challenges of starting a Twelve Step-oriented group devoted to a particular Behavioral Addiction is Chapter 7, "Starting an S.L.A.A. Group" in S.L.A.A.'s basic text *Sex and Love Addicts Anonymous.* This chapter sets forth in considerable detail the likely evolutionary challenges you will face in starting a group, along with time-tested suggestions for recognizing and mastering these challenges as they start to unfold.
34. Also (I say this tongue-in-cheek) your therapist or counselor may learn a thing or two!

Perspectives on Diagnosing and Treating Behavioral Addictions in Others

In professional settings, meaning in-patient addiction treatment programs, psychiatric units in general hospitals, detox units (usually consisting of very short-term, "spin-dry" regimens), outpatient programs connected to clinics, and private practice outpatient settings, the major dilemma, right up front, is:

"To diagnose and treat, or NOT to diagnose and treat?—That is the question."

Here are some typical challenges to diagnosing Behavioral Addictions in various treatment settings:

(1) The existence of Behavioral Addictions is not all that recognized in the field of addictions treatment.

(2) Often diagnoses don't qualify for third-party reimbursement due to the diagnostic nomenclature of the DSM.[35]

---

35. In DSM-IV there were some workarounds (sort of) for dealing with the limitations of DSM-IV. Such categories as Pathological Gambling (under Impulsive Control Disorder Not Otherwise Specified), Binge Eating disorder (mentioned in DSM-IV as a diagnosis for further study), Sexual Disorder—listed under Paraphilias (some quite specific, as in "Exhibitionism," or Paraphilia NOS (Not Otherwise Specified), and Pathological Lying (under Antisocial Personality Disorder) could be distended into service, after a fashion. In DSM-V, under the heading "Substance-Related and Addictive Disorders," only "gambling disorder" has achieved stand-alone status as a diagnosable Behavioral Addiction. In a section outlining "conditions" slated for "further research" one finds only "internet gaming disorder" listed—and

(3) Within a treatment setting, there is often a lack of institutional support for such diagnoses. Administratively, this lack of support can be both clinical—due to the trail-blazing quality of these diagnoses that refuse to be demurely folded into the diagnostic categories and nomenclature of the DSM and rightfully demand their own, addictions-oriented treatment approaches—and also administrative, involving issues of coding and reimbursability of Behavioral Addictions diagnoses, as well as funding considerations regarding qualifying for federal, state and community programs and resources.

(4) If you're working as an addictions counselor in a primarily mental health-oriented treatment setting (such as a community mental health center or a private treatment hospital for mental disorders), it is typical for some symptoms of the criteria you use (the Five Diagnostic Criteria) for diagnosing a Behavioral Addiction to be construed as falling under the purview of other "mental disorder" diagnostic categories within the DSM. Therefore you may find your own readiness to engage in treatment

---

not currently diagnosable. Addictions that pertain to sex, "love" (morbid dependency), compulsive overeating and other eating disorders, kleptomania, rage, etc., are absent as listed addictions in DSM-V, either as diagnosable or syndromes slated for "further study." Possibly, some workarounds may exist in coding de facto Behavioral Addictions under the headings "Obsessive-Compulsive and Related Disorders," and "Adjustment Disorders," "Anxiety Disorders" in DSM-V. If you're creative, you can likely come up with other workarounds for the deficiencies of DSM-V. If you're heeding the Five Diagnostic Criteria in making your diagnosis of a Behavioral Addiction, know that the shortcoming resides in the DSM nomenclature and the competitive process behind it, rather than with your own diagnostic skills.

with your Behavioral Addictions-prone client to be peremptorily undercut, with the client being referred to a mental health clinician (who likely has little if any background in addictions theory, diagnosis and treatment).

(5) There is no current licensure of a comprehensive nature in effect for Behavioral Addictions.[36]

A conclusion we might draw from these five points is that if you diagnose a Behavioral Addiction as a primary (or even strong secondary) diagnosis, in the absence of institutional support and a recognized diagnostic framework, you'll likely be sticking your neck out. So, one must proceed with a degree

---

36. As of this writing there is no licensure for Behavioral Addictions practitioners. The professional field of addictions treatment has, for decades now, been preoccupied almost exclusively with the realms of alcoholism and drug addiction, and hardly recognizes the relevance of Behavioral Addictions, with the possible exception of compulsive gambling. In the gambling area, certification exists, but no licensure. The trend in the overall addictions treatment field seems to be to further fragment, split-off and demarcate ever more specific areas of *particular* addictions. This is lamentable and short-sighted, often a product of attempting to define and "own" treatment turf (with primary attention paid to reimbursability and program funding), rather than being motivated by concern for patient wellbeing or the appropriate, future development of the overall addictions treatment field. Given the underlying dynamics of addiction—the Five Diagnostic Criteria—which pertain to, and define, all addictions as an *encompassing* phenomenon, it will be folly if obtaining specific licensure(s) and certifications becomes the official requirement for being able to engage in clinical practice with clients with "specific" addictions, rather than a single license or certification that qualifies a practitioner to practice, with highly transferable skills, throughout the encompassing sphere that addiction *is*.

of caution, notwithstanding clinical observations that may be compelling and "obvious" to you as to their diagnostic and prognostic relevance. One must accept the informal role of educating one's colleagues regarding diagnosis and treatment not just of Behavioral Addictions, but of the substance-based ones as well. You will develop clinical credibility as you proceed with your own casework, augmented by your own respectful, constructive comments regarding your colleagues' casework.

Here are the clinical caveats for diagnosing Behavioral Addictions in your work setting. First, in a spirit of clinical caution, here are a few guidelines for when the diagnosis of Behavioral Addictions is *contraindicated,* despite clear evidence of their presence:

(1) Regarding persons who are newly sober/clean in terms of alcohol/substances, the strong component of personal identity that Behavioral Addictions supply makes then "too much" to deal with in early recovery for alcoholics and drug addicts, even if you're right about what you think you're seeing in such a client.

(2) To press ahead in such circumstances is to risk pushing the client into a psychotic break/identity collapse—a "nervous breakdown" (as it used to be called), in which a center of personal identity capable of processing new information—and new challenges—fragments, and is no longer able to absorb and digest "pertinent truths" that may have been, diagnostically, newly discovered by the therapist.

And . . . here is the one guideline in which making a diagnosis of a Behavioral Addiction is *mandatory* in a newly sober/clean alcoholic/drug addict:

(3) The ONE EXCEPTION, when early diagnosis IS warranted, is in the circumstance where the client has *a chronic, documented pattern of alcohol/substance abuse relapse, and the pattern of relapse appears linked to the presence of, and acting out on, a Behavioral Addiction.* For instance, a chronic history of drug/alcohol relapse *linked directly* to relationships, or breakups, or harassment by creditors, or legal difficulties due to alleged assaults, etc., are all indicators of an undiagnosed Behavioral Addiction torpedoing being "clean and sober." If such a history exists, you may have to ferret it out with your client. Sometimes the history is obvious; other times it is hidden. Good interviewing skills come into play here.

Re: "triaging" cases combining both alcoholism/drug addiction and one or more Behavioral Addictions

In cases, more the rule than the exception, in which a person is referred into treatment or, as happens sometimes, comes in on their own free will and initiative, and "presents," along with symptoms of active alcoholism and/or drug addiction, an array of thoroughly suspect behaviors consistent with the likely presence of one or more Behavioral Addictions, it can be helpful to adopt a strategy of *triage* regarding all that is being presented.

The abiding question that can lead to some smart, and timely, triaging goes as follows:

(1) In this newly sober/clean or alcohol-/drug-addicted person sitting before me, assuming that what I am "seeing," in terms of the active presence of Behavioral Addictions is correct, *what among these still-active addictions will kill, or lead to unmanageability in, this person* ***the quickest?***

(2) The guideline is: Address whatever the Behavioral Addiction is that can more immediately sabotage early recovery, and TOLERATE the ones that aren't presently as dire, even if you see trouble brewing with them down the road.

Regarding this latter point, bear in mind that it's entirely possible that you are correct about what you're seeing, and *could* be diagnosing. However, if your client is "clean and sober" in term of alcohol and drugs, and is committed to their recovery, that person, even in the presence of still active Behavioral Addictions, is nonetheless starting to gain a toehold into sober life. In other words, their identity, although still involved with, and partially fashioned by, ongoing destructive behaviors, is starting to be remade in a manner that, in the fullness of time, will be stable and firm enough to withstand the loss-of-personal-identity challenges that accompany coming to terms with any addiction.

It's also worth noting that in in-patient specialized addictions units (which are usually aimed at detoxing and treating active alcoholics and drug addicts), every once in a while a person will seek admittance into such a program with the presenting complaint, not of alcoholism or drug addiction, but, rather, a Behavioral Addiction. This is rare, but it *does* happen. From a clinical standpoint this can be a nice turn of events. Recalling our own professional field's origins in the grass-roots stew of self-help groups and, especially, the meaningfulness of "self-diagnosis," such a client is a latter-day example of what has been the provenance of the whole addictions treatment field: someone "noticing" something, being increasingly troubled by that "something," and then, tentatively—although never without courage—daring to "self-diagnose" on the basis of that "something." Exploring the ramifications of that troubling "something," using the terms and concepts that the person has come up with on their own, is the way to go here. Through their eyes we witness the miracle of emerging self-awareness, and there is, in a way, nothing for us, as professionals, to "correct." We can sit with, listen, and gently encourage the seeds of recovery that are already taking root.

Further principles on treating Behavioral Addictions

The best combination of strategies—if available—for treating Behavioral Addictions has an old familiar ring to it. There are no surprises here, for, from the standpoint of Addiction Energy, addiction is addiction, period. So (no surprise) the "best combination" is active involvement with a Twelve-Step fellowship specific to that Behavioral Addiction (if one exists), plus professional counseling.

"Hitch-hiking" on other related Twelve-Step fellowships is one way to go if a fellowship specific to a given Behavioral Addiction is not in existence or otherwise available. This attempt at finding one's "sea legs" in a fellowship that is differently directed in terms of its "primary purpose" is not, as previously mentioned, without difficulty or challenge. The prevailing culture of any Twelve-Step fellowship will be a product of what it seeks to address. Those whose addictions may be seemingly at odds with the group's "primary purpose" can be perceived as "different," and therefore not as readily welcomed or accepted as the regular flock. Taking all this into consideration, the pluses of being in the presence of a self-help, mutual aid fellowship (such as the ones oriented around A.A.'s Twelve Steps), still outweigh the minuses. In this case, "something" in the self-help/mutual aid arena is better than "nothing," because, just as with drug addiction and alcoholism, *the prognosis for recovery using, and relying upon, counseling or psychotherapy alone is poor.*

In-patient (residential) programs do exist for some of the Behavioral Addictions (as in the hybrid addiction of compulsive overeating and other eating disorders, self-harm, sex addiction, "love" addiction, etc.) and they can be very helpful in establishing a safe setting for a person to enter elective withdrawal. However, sometimes these programs promote themselves in a manner that can appear quite enticing—seductive, even—as in being "the answer" for (such-and-such) addiction—implying that they are capable of delivering more than may be possible in a given situation. Bear in mind that such programs and "recovery centers" are usually commercial enterprises seeking to survive, and profit, in a competitive commercial environment. They all have marketing departments to tailor and spread the message to the would-be faithful. It's worth noting that "at the end of the day"—meaning at the time of treatment discharge (after all those hefty fees have been chalked up, and insurance payments have been exhausted)—the "treatment recommendations" for ALL clients remain substantially the same: involvement in a Twelve-Step-oriented self-help fellowship, combined with some form of outpatient counseling or group therapy.

On inpatient units that are (as most are) directed primarily to treatment of alcoholism and drug addiction, there is still the possibility of doing something creative, vis-à-vis Behavioral Addictions. One idea is to establish, as a part of regular treatment, a range of "special purpose" groups on the unit that can address a swath of related behaviors which (off the record) could loosely qualify as a category of addiction. These groups need not be cast too narrowly. For instance, detoxing alcoholics and drug addicts who have relapse histories combined with gambling, compulsive indebtedness or compulsive spending, etc., could take part in a "money problems" group. Ditto: "shame group," "anger issues group," "relationships group," "video gaming issues group," "online pornography issues group," and so on. These groups, as professionally facilitated, would not have the goal of diagnosing Behavioral Addictions per se. They would, however, be very useful in providing a supportive climate, in which issues, and resources, that could relate to the possible presence of Behavioral Addictions in attendees could be more openly discussed in a non-judgmental environment.

As a result of attending one or more of these groups, group attendees would have the option (in a spirit of self-diagnosis) to discuss further with their regular case counselor on the unit whatever fresh awarenesses pertaining to some specific category of behavior may have caught their attention.

Another concept that has proven useful in understanding the more extended process that so many newly sober and clean alcoholics and drug addicts start to be confronted with in the course of their evolving recoveries is called the "LIFO" ("Last In, First Out") concept[37]. The principle here is that Behavioral Addictions (whatever they may be) that *precede* substance-based addictions in the life of an alcoholic or drug addict will tend to resurface in the recovery of sober alcoholics and drug addicts in the *reverse* order—in the opposite order—in which they were acquired. In other words, the "most recent" acquisitions will be the first to manifest in the life of the recovering alcoholic and drug addict. Longer term—and therefore more deep-seated—Behavioral Addictions will likely come to the surface later (sometimes much later) in recovery.

These addictions, and the sequence in which they show up in the life of the recovering addict/alcoholic, will comprise the unfolding challenges to, and milestones of, longer-term recovery. Therefore, if at all possible, it is worthwhile gathering enough information, by way of a "case history," to make some sort of

37. The "LIFO" ("Last In, First Out") concept mentioned above actually has its provenance in the world of professional accounting, as a guideline to be followed by businesses in handling reportable income and expenses. This concept transfers with uncanny, predictive utility into the realm of addiction diagnosis and treatment.

educated guess as to whether or not Behavioral Addictions exist in the earlier history of your client. If so, those are the ones that may be currently latent, but will likely "slumber awake" at some point.

If the counselor is aware of a preceding history of Behavioral Addictions in their client, the counselor can begin to assist their client in learning about the possibility of there being "Second Surrenders" as an *expected* part of longer-term recovery. By "expected," one does not mean mandated to be dealt with by some external moral or legal authority. Rather, "expected" means a gradual surfacing of something that gets one's notice, and becomes troublesome enough that the person *wants* to deal with it. Despite situational trials and tribulations, and, perhaps, destructive behavior and poor judgment stemming from manifestations of Behavioral Addictions in recovery, the person (your client, in this case) has not, *in the larger sense,* "done anything wrong," or, terminally "screwed up." All of this is just part and parcel of what longer- and long-term recovery consists of, and, in coming to terms with it—"little by slow"—one is, short of irrevocable, unconditional sabotage in the form of alcohol and drug relapse—still "on the path."

This overall concept of "Second Surrenders" warrants further comment. It is a powerful reality in the life of so many recovering addicts and alcoholics that the initial surrender to being powerless over one's drinking or drugging, monumental as that surrender may be, is, in the overall scheme of things, just the first of what, in the fullness of time, becomes a *sequence of surrenders,* as Behavioral Addictions start to take their toll in recovery, and the recovering person becomes more capable, over time, of facing them. Subsequent surrenders are often years apart from one another, as the cumulative amassing of a larger life-experience in recovery gradually brings them into focus as something that must be dealt with. As mentioned previously in this book, over the much longer timeframe of recovery, it seems likely that what commences as a limited, although difficult, surrender regarding alcohol and drugs, becomes, very gradually, through a progression of widely-spaced subsequent surrenders, a full surrender to life as a human being.

Some thoughts about *outpatient* treatment of alcoholics and drug addicts in early recovery

What follows are a few comments aimed at those counselors whose work is primarily with clinical outpatients. First, there is less leverage available in an outpatient setting than on an inpatient unit. The inpatient unit has, to some extent, a "captive audience," temporarily removed from the thousand fragmenting influences of the hurly-burly of everyday life. Not so in outpatient counseling. Your office, or setting, may be, at times, an oasis, sanctuary, or refuge of sorts, but it is so ephemeral, and easily cast aside under the onslaught of situational dynamics awaiting your client just outside your door. Also, it is not at all unusual, in the managed care environment, that only a limited number of sessions have been authorized for your client(s). So, very little time may be available for anything cumulative to take hold in outpatient work.

There are exceptions to this. Sometimes clients may seek further sessions and these may be approved—although even in this instance they usually have to be justified in terms of meeting specific, short-term treatment goals. It is not at all unusual to have to attempt to justify extension of sessions in clinical terms that are deemed not relevant to the managed care case reviewer. There are so many instances in which the supposed "managed care" function is really, de facto, double-speak for "denial of access." There are also those rarer occasions where clients find outpatient counseling of such value that, once benefits (session "approvals") are expended, they may seek to continue on at their own expense. Whether functioning as a clinician in a mental health clinic, or working through one's own private practice, establishing a "sliding scale" option for these folks is, arguably, morally and ethically necessary and justifiable.

Nevertheless, under these trying conditions it is *still possible* to start to foster awareness, in one's client, about what may eventually need to be faced and dealt with—to some extent normalizing this process of "ongoing surrenders." One should not try to force awareness of such possibilities on one's client. As is true for all of us, a person can tolerate only a finite amount of consciousness-raising at any given time. Yet, in planting the seed that a phenomenon called "Second Surrender" exists in the lives of many recovering people; in educating your client that this phenomenon relates to awarenesses that come to mind as a result of ongoing life-experiences in recovery—that there is no "rushing" these recognitions, as they are likely to surface over time as a person is more ready, and capable, to both see them and work with them—a sense of *normalizing* the progression of these events can start to be factored into the mental, emotional and spiritual calculus of those who are embarking on their odyssey of recovery.

CHAPTER NINE

Reframing Recovery:

A Different 'Vision for You': Promises of Recovery vs. Adventures of Discovery

Whether you're working in a treatment center that specializes in addressing Behavioral Addictions (few and far between); or in an addictions treatment center that focuses on alcoholism and drug addiction (but where, on occasion, a diagnosis is correctly made regarding the co-presence of a Behavioral Addiction as a matter that needs to be addressed during the inpatient stay); or working in outpatient settings (clinic or private practice) in which there is ongoing counseling regarding Behavioral Addictions *as a component of what it is proper to address as an "addictions treatment professional"*; or . . . if you are one of those who are already living out their lives as recovering alcoholics and drug addicts and have been successful, one day at a time, in establishing a foundation in recovery—in each, and all, of these settings and circumstances it can be highly useful to reframe what the task is, and qualities are, either for your client, or for yourself (whichever applies)—for whoever is facing the challenge of coming to grips with these additional (addictional) afflictions.

The apparent reality is that even with the obsession and

compulsion of active alcoholism and drug addiction removed, or held in abeyance (whether one calls this reprieve or remission), Addiction Energy—the *ENERGY!!*—that amazing amalgam of forces that underlies all addictions—continues to exist, and, at times, can surface in ways that risk being highly destructive. As has already been made clear, against this seemingly immovable backdrop of the persistence of Addiction Energy, what the longer-term picture looks like for so many is the sequential unfolding of various Behavioral Addictions that, in turn, lead, over an arc of years, to subsequent surrenders: 2nd . . . 3nd . . . 4th . . . nth . . . So much for arrival in a once-and-for-all "happy, joyous and free" condition as some semi-permanent steady-state reality in recovery!

I gently state, once again, that when Bill W., A.A.'s co-founder, wrote the "Promises" (pages 83–84 in *Alcoholics Anonymous*), he was likely sober no more than two and a half years. While that sobriety was a remarkable achievement, the simple truth is that he was not sober long enough—had not yet amassed enough sober experience—to truly know what the bigger, longer-term picture was, and is, for those in recovery. As I've mentioned earlier, while Bill W.'s greatness as a trail-blazing pioneer and visionary is undeniable, I have, very informally (since realizing the time-line involved), come to refer to the "Promises" as "Bill W.'s earnest hopes."[38]

---

38. The Big Book "Promises," written in 1937 or so, are visionary statements of, as yet, unrealized possibilities. They are mostly set forth in the future tense. The language, though declarative and hopeful, is speculative. This contrasts tremendously with the culminating paragraphs in the "Step Twelve" chapter of the *Twelve & Twelve*, written some 14 years later. In the two

So . . . against this much more sober, and sobering, reality of multiple (2nd . . . 3nd . . . 4th . . . nth . . . .) surrenders, all, in the fullness of time, made necessary by the continuous out-workings of Addiction Energy, what is there that can be said about this ongoing process which can lend it any kind of hopeful and meaningful realization? The rest of this chapter seeks to address this question.

"Promises of Recovery" vs. "Adventures of Discovery"

The crucial point in reframing what it is to work with Behavioral Addictions, whether within oneself or with someone else, is to come to a recognition that the challenge is not simply that of stopping a destructive behavior and steeling oneself to get through a period of deprivation (i.e. "withdrawal" from "acting out"). Rather, *the deeper challenge is that of taking a chance on the unknown.* In initially ceasing a particular destructive behavior, one is necessarily drawn more deeply into dealing with *patterns* of destructive behavior. What may, at the outset, be an

---

ultimate paragraphs of this chapter (pages 124–125), the language of what recovery yields is the language of proven experience, expressed in the present tense, and the words used to describe these realizations are the words of deep knowing —of attainments *realized.* These words include: "feeling," "knowledge," "well understood fact," "proof," "certainty," and "surety." The language, and the sentiments contained therein, reveal that Bill W.'s own odyssey had progressed, through his own subsequent surrenders in recovery, from early visionary and idealist, to grounded, redeemed realist—as "one who truly knows" in a manner that only experience-at-depth can provide.

"impulse to quit" as a reflexive, impulsive, perhaps desperate act due to encountering some extremely painful or frightening consequence of acting out, reveals, soon enough, that the larger issue is not simply the most recent misdeed or episode, but, rather, *a whole pattern of destructive behavior*—one's destructive behavioral signature, so to speak. In short: one's personal identity.

This places "quitting" in a whole different context. Rather than "stopping," and, with teeth clenched, white-knuckling oneself into "staying stopped," the authentic, true inner drama (in the best sense of the word) becomes: *daring to face an unknown Self.*

This takes tremendous courage. If a person has, through the progression of their acting-out history with Behavioral Addictions, come to the point of experiencing authentic terror and despair—the *experience* of one's sanity (what's left of it) being in free-fall, soon to be gone and forever beyond retrieval—*that* sure consequence of continuing on with their addictive behavior becomes a gut-wrenching, terrifying prospect. It's all the more terrifying when this sense of desperation is heightened by the further awareness, usually borne out in one's personal history, that even in the heat of a keen awareness about how desperate "my" actual situation is, "I" am still utterly unable to know *if* "I" can stop. Amnesia as to the direness of one's plight may set in once again (as it so often does), leading to a brief respite from terror's onslaught, but the resumption of addictive activity will once again see terror crashing through the false ceiling of security that "forgetfulness" may, so ephemerally, supply. So . . . *Option One*—

that of continuing—becomes too horrible to knowingly choose.

Short of suicide, which only concretizes "stopping" in a most garish and grotesque way—only manages to accomplish bodily/physically what, in essence, needs to be a psychological, emotional and spiritual victory—*Option Two: facing one's unknown Self,* is the only option left. And, Option Two, "facing the unknown Self," usually feels, *almost,* ***but not quite***, as desperate and as terrifying a prospect as not stopping the addiction at all. In other words, it is a courageous act to embark on such a course, no matter how necessary it may be to do so, in the absence of there being any guarantees regarding outcome.

Therefore, the first reframing of what it is to "take on" and grapple with coming to terms with a Behavioral Addiction, is that one risks facing an unknown Self, with no guarantee of outcome, and . . . it takes great courage to do so.

This gets to the second bit of reframing what is at stake here. *The "Promises," as glowing and visionary as they may be, do not pertain in any assured way to tackling a Behavioral Addiction.* Some qualities of these celebrated promises, or perhaps all (if a person is really both blessed and fortunate), may arise in the course of following the difficult path of facing an unknown Self, but . . . these qualities (the Promises) are not really able to be "promises." They may be possibilities, but they cannot be guaranteed. *Because no one who is at the jumping-off point prior to facing a Behavioral Addiction can actually know what (or whom) he or she is really facing in this process, there is only one certainty, and it is this: "Promises of Recovery" have to give way, somewhat, to "Adventures of Personal Discovery."*

Indeed, *for someone who is faced with embarking on this challenging path, the welling up of the courage it takes to enter, and stick to, this course, may be the first attribute of an "unknown Self" to surface.* The use of the term "heroic" to characterize the nature of this journey is no exaggeration. Anyone who embarks on it can, from the moment of this journey's inception, claim, and feel, their own personal courage and heroism.

Because of the individual nature of this process of "meeting the unknown Self," it is not possible to set the process forth as some kind of blueprint to follow. Those people who are actively in recovery in A.A. or N.A., and/or have found a Twelve Step fellowship more specifically addressing the Behavioral Addiction in question, will, of course, continue their involvement in these fellowships, and especially their "step work," in whatever fashion feels most helpful to them. There is so much in the Twelve Steps that can be helpful. Those who buttress their self-help group involvement with counseling or psychotherapy will also find these settings of considerable value in discussing new "discoveries" and inner, as well as outer, "encounters." *Ultimately*, however, the path to *"meeting the unknown Self"*—eventually coming into resonance with this reality (in which the "unknown Self" becomes, over time, increasing "known," and the person who "I" think I am eventually grows into a correspondence with this "other side of me" and, in the fullness of time, starts to become *blended* with it)—*is an **individual** adventure*, rather than a collective one. Fellowship is helpful, and the network of support fellowship offers is priceless, but . . . unto itself fellowship is always a collective, or group experience, while *this journey of finding* *(or being found by), establishing relations with, and, ultimately, befriending—both assimilating, and being assimilated by—the "other," eventually realizing a "shared" identity in which the "other" increasingly feels like ME—is always, at its roots, personal and individual.*

In the absence of a blueprint to follow entitled something like: "How to do the proper adventure of self-confrontation," I am able to offer brief comments on what the adventure, over time, may yield for people who face the challenge of meeting the unknown Self.

For men specifically, there is the experience of discovering the *real* foundations of one's manhood. Risking this journey, rather than continuing to live destructively (with only a tragic, toxic, pathetic legacy to show for it) is an act of true courage. Once the connection is made between one's own manhood and the courage it takes to undergo the adventures of self-discovery, *that* quality of courage comes to rule as the gold standard for what manhood *is*. Collective standards and values revolving around sexual exploitation, violence, abuse, power, sadism, cruelty, "action," conspicuous consumption, the philosophy of "Whoever dies with the most toys, wins," along with so many other collective, lower common-denominator values which lull unsuspecting men onto the path of polluted and unworthy pursuits—and provide unaddressed Addiction Energy with an endless playground for manifestation—start to fall by the wayside. *Within, something of incomparably greater value has been minted, and comes to be cherished.*

For women, coming to deal with a Behavioral Addiction, and risking the inner journey of "meeting the unknown Self," can result, over time, in becoming a more integrated and powerful person, less susceptible to the negative influence of gender stereotypes and other cultural pressures (about how to look, how to act, what to own). Women in recovery from Behavioral Addictions gradually become less dependent on external attitudes and forces, other than those which promote their own wellbeing, and the wellbeing of others around them. They become less likely to fall victim to sexual and other forms of exploitation. As one comes to relate positively to the Self, relationships with others also improve. The journey is towards a life of greater fulfillment, relatively unencumbered by social strictures or the expectations of other people, even including, at times, those of family and friends.

In short, *choices that were made impulsively and unconsciously, now made clearly discernible through the process of "meeting the unknown Self," are repudiated, and conscious decision-making becomes more the norm. This is a gateway to personal dignity and freedom.*

While these comments on some of the dividends that men and women have realized through this process are parsed by gender, there is plenty of shared territory on the road to "personhood." One of the largest shared tracts for both women and men—for *everyone* who goes through this process—is the changing of how those in recovery come to see themselves in relation to the culture-at-large. Because our culture (especially in the U.S., but equally true in many countries around the world), in its collective ignorance, promotes, under drive for profit, power, success, and "the good life," many behavioral gateways that, in the addiction-prone, develop into Behavioral

Addictions, at the individual level it is really not possible to explore personal recovery in the Behavioral Addictions realm without, sooner or later, coming to question one's relationship to the culture-at-large. From the standpoint of personal recovery, the pathologies of societal ignorance and folly are everywhere in abundance. For those in recovery, they become so apparent and obvious—and painful to witness.

Nevertheless, since all those in recovery are obliged to continue to exist within the context of their society and culture, the common thread of outcome to this challenge is to detach from what is toxic, and, in some way, usher into the world (usually at the level of one's immediate environment) an energy of relative sanity. In other words, from the standpoint of recovery, what society "needs," is, at the micro-level, something that those in recovery, through the very realization and easy manifestation of their new reality, are able to provide. Each recovering person, whether male or female, transgender, gay, lesbian, straight, queer, is, in the context of their own life circumstances, now, through their mere presence, in a very informal yet profound way, a channel for a healing possibility, already being realized on the personal level. With growing numbers of people in recovery, the arising of "sanity," at the societal level, as engendered by a broadening current of transformation born of numerous personal transformations and healing, although seemingly a long shot, is not categorically forever beyond possibility.

A few final thoughts on the ramifications of "Adventures in Personal Discovery"

In the multi-millennial history of homo sapiens (approximately 200,000 years or so), all possible combinations and permutations of human tragedy, violence, destructiveness, degradation, self-defilement, and disgust have been lived out over and over again—countless billions of times. Humiliations, innumerable cruelties, behaviors—both wantonly reckless and exploitative—incalculable acts of senseless violence and mayhem, mass murders (along with an endless procession of individual ones), have abounded in the recorded history, and pre-history, of the human species.

In awakening to the reality of human history as largely consisting of a seemingly bottomless cesspool of folly, greed, corruptibility, violence, tragedy and mayhem, one comes to recognize that *there are no new, nor novel, chapters in suffering, degradation and misery remaining to be lived. They have all been done. Fini.*

There are, however, untold adventures, both newly minted and novel, in recovery and wellness to be lived out. They are all unique, individual adventures and they cannot be duplicated. They have never been lived before, in exactly the same way, as they transpire in the life of one who embarks on the journey of "meeting the unknown Self," and lives it through to the end. Apparently, there are no defined upper limits of "arrival" to these adventures, as this territory, throughout human history, has been largely virginal, trackless, rich in potential, and, thus far, almost completely unexplored.

It is at this intersection between human suffering—in the form of addictions generally, and Behavioral Addictions in particular—and the imperative, born first of the need to survive—to find an path up and out of such pathological workings and their sorry legacy—*and then to prosper,* that this far-reaching adventure of the human spirit finds its strength to venture into the unknown. Beyond the cessation of pointless, repetitious, destructive acts—and with no other guarantees regarding assured outcomes—one harkens to the possibility of a better world, beginning with the dignity of individual recovery, one person, one day, and one adventure at a time.

CHAPTER TEN

Concerning One's 'Ultimate' Relationship with Addiction Energy

In Recovery: How Healed Is It Possible to Become?

It is time to return to the topic of Addiction Energy—the *ENERGY!!*. We've been on quite an excursion, seemingly venturing far away from it. From presenting some case vignettes demonstrating how Behavioral Addictions can precede, coincide with, or develop subsequent to substance-based addictions; then on into considerations around self- and clinical diagnosis and treatment of Behavioral Addictions, including the unfolding of subsequent "surrenders"; and, finally, reframing recovery as a series of adventures in self-discovery rather than promises of assured outcomes, relatively few specific mentions, through these later chapters, have been made, along the way, of "Addiction Energy."

So now it's time to take this topic up again . . . for it has never really left us.

And, from what appears to be the case, Addiction Energy—the *ENERGY!!*— in all its displaceable glory, *doesn't* leave us.

It seems as if its presence remains a "given," regardless of length of recovery, ferventness of devotion to recovery, and all attempts, no matter how well-grounded they may seem and how thoroughly regaled they are with earnest yearnings and honest efforts, to be rid, or free, of it.

This is difficult, indeed, to reconcile. In our world of linear thinking and rational sensemaking, honest efforts should be met with honest rewards. If we're trying hard, we should be successful. If we're "doing God's work," we should be divinely protected and "delivered from evil." If we're of noble character and possessed of utopian visions, focused efforts should be sufficient to bring them into manifestation. It just ain't fair that it ain't necessarily so!!

The question that arises is: If Addiction Energy—the *ENERGY!!*—remains in the mix of who we are and what comprises us, where does that ultimately leave us? Indeed, under such circumstances what does "healing" even mean? This is a riddle that evades facile resolution. Rather, the best I can offer, the limited products of over forty years of intense involvement, both personal and as a professional, with the realm of Behavioral Addictions, is to present a *range* of possibilities, or options, that may shed a bit of light on this whole question. It is possible that each one of these options carries some resonance of healing to it. They all fall far short of a once-and-for-all final fix, but they *do* provide grounded hope that a life "lived to good purpose, always," remains an attainable reality, notwithstanding the lack of complete (in conventional terms) healing.

So . . . here is a range of possibilities:

(1) Being *removed* from the "Energy"/the "Energy" is *removed*. This is the old exorcism model earlier discussed. It can be attempted either within a religious context, or through employing a secular procedure of some sort. However, while it can't be claimed that exorcism, either religious or secular, is never successful in its effects, I have yet to witness a completely delivered healing outcome from this approach. The tease is that, regarding a specific behavioral addiction, obsession and compulsion may, indeed, "take a hike," rendering the impression that cure is at hand. But, in the larger scheme of things, Addiction Energy waits in the wings, bides its time, and subsequently erupts in some different area of behavior.

(2) Being *cleared* of the Energy. This is a variation on the exorcism approach, a bit like attempting to "clear" a house of ghosts by burning sage in the various rooms (accompanied, perhaps, by incantations of one sort or another)—or clearing my "magic slate" toy of childhood by peeling up the transparent membrane. This "sage" method has reportedly been effective in "clearing" physical spaces of apparitions and hauntings, but it has not, to my knowledge, proven effective in "clearing" Addiction Energy from the human body.

(3) Being released from being held in bondage by the Energy. At first glance this would appear to be taking another shot at an exorcism cure, but it is really more nuanced than that. Being free of being held in bondage by the Energy does *not* necessarily mean that the Energy is not still there—only that one is not held in its thrall. In fact, *it **is** possible to be free*

of Addiction Energy's bondage despite the ongoing presence of the Energy, rather than having a condition of relative freedom dependent entirely on the Energy's no longer being in the mix.

(4) Being *restored to sanity* regarding the Energy. "Sanity" is a legal term, rather than a psychological one. It carries overtones of "sound thinking," and being able to function within societal norms—i.e., not getting into trouble. It is not a glorious, uplifting standard, but one that is immensely practical. To have attained "sanity" in the addictions sphere means that a person is in touch with what can, as an ongoing presence, continue to bedevil him—and *will*, if not carefully attended to. *Clarity of mind, in the presence of that which can overthrow it, is a tremendous acquisition.* It is foundational to whatever life-edifice can be constructed upon it. Curiously, there is nothing about "sanity" that assumes that the roots of insanity have been extirpated, or vanquished. Within the purview of Addiction Energy, "sanity" is always under assault, either blatant or subtle. *It would seem that it is the act of being under assault that pushes "sanity" to continue to upgrade the bolstering of its own defenses, thereby keeping it robust in the face of being challenged.* This, as first glance, may not seem like a great healing outcome, but considering the alternative, one could do far worse.

(5) *Surrender to the reality of the Energy.* Surrender means many things in the addictions treatment world. It can mean "surrendering" to the reality that "I" cannot indulge (imbibe, consume, inject, inhale, snort, act-out) in safety (in whatever form of addiction is bedeviling me). It can also mean taking

the profound step *away* from acting out—meaning not merely cessation of "using" due to some recent jackpot or calamity, but, rather, turning away from a whole *pattern*—often decades long—of wanton indulgence. Recovery often has its roots in these two levels of "surrender."

There is, however, a third level of surrender that may take longer to grasp, and hews, perhaps, closer to a truth that all those who are recovering, or would embark on recovery, come to face, in some form, sooner or later. It is this: *Addiction, and the* energy *that underlies, infuses, and suffuses it in all its forms, are **objective** realities that exist independent of human will and volition.* Addiction Energy, and its many outworkings (so destructive in their untreated, unengaged form) exist as an independent variable, apart from human-scale life. The *ENERGY!!* exists independent of humanity's collective will that it not exist. As the saying (within the addictions treatment world) goes, "I can choose to forget about (my) addiction, but (my) addiction will not forget about me."

In surrendering to the recognition of the objective reality of Addiction Energy's existence, one may feel a pang of existential unknowing as to why this is so. Perhaps the healing that comes out of such an awareness relates to a wonderfully worded passage from the Step Eleven chapter in the *Twelve & Twelve* (page 103). In it, Bill W. is opining about a certain outlook that can sometimes break the logjam of "anger, fear, frustration and misunderstanding." His wording here is subtle and ingenious. Rather than coming up with a nostrum about achieving relief and solace through the *finding* of God's will, he says, instead, that "the surest help of all" is not, per se, a definitive finding of God's will for us, but *arises in the process of "our search for it."* For those who are philosophically inclined, the commitment to such a search, as "the surest help of all" may hold a considerable dimension of healing.

(6) *Becoming reconciled with the Energy* (and with oneself for hosting it). Reconciliation hints at there being a level of mutual engagement between two previously estranged, or alienated, parties. In the Behavioral Addictions realm (and, likely, in all the substance-based manifestations of addiction as well), the two estranged components are "me," in ego-identity form—who does not "want to be like this or doing these kinds of things or creating this kind of damage"—and Addiction Energy (however one may experience or personify it) which, in ways both mysterious and blatant, forces "me" to seek oblivion and visit destruction on my life and the lives of others. So . . . at a very base level, "reconciling" means two things: first, coming to terms with the objective reality of Addiction Energy as an ongoing presence in one's life, leading, in some curious way, to a *felt* comprehension that Addiction Energy has a "right to be here," and, second, reconciling with that part of "me" that is obviously capable of hosting this energy: in short, forgiving myself for "having it." While both recognitions—the objective reality of Addiction Energy/its right to exist, and the need to enter into some self-forgiveness for "having it"—may leave one in a doleful frame of mind, Addiction Energy that is (after a fashion) acknowledged as having a rightful claim on being in the mix of who "I" am may, as a result of finally being accepted, have a more instructive and

fruitful face to show than mere destructiveness, and the side of "me" that hosts it can come in, a bit, from the cold of having been alienated, cast out, or exiled, into a fuller participation in my ("our") collective, internal reality. From the origins of such humble recognitions, further possibilities exist as to what can develop in the healing realm.

(7) *Coexisting (co-exisitng) with the Energy* (as necessary). To coexist (co-exist) literally means two "something's" that are *mutually* existing, and are forced to accept each other's existence because neither can banish, or be banished by, the other. This is the "grudging" form of coexistence—and often the basis on which coexistence is initially arrived at. From humble, begrudged origins like this, however, coexistence can expand beyond mere resignation and toleration. At a minimum, coexistence means that Addiction Energy's presence in our lives is taken as a *given*, a structural reality that, in its origins, is NOT a result of our having screwed up or otherwise caused. In a sense, it's "where we find ourselves," both colloquially and literally. The great gift stemming from coming to terms with the coexistence reality is that living a life "to good purpose, always," need not be dependent on Addiction Energy's being vanquished, defeated, or otherwise exorcised or subdued. As already mentioned, *a life can be, on balance, positive and affirming of values of love and non-destructiveness even in the ongoing presence of Addiction Energy.* One can think of the ongoing presence of Addiction Energy as certain "tendencies" that a person has which are life-long. Behaviors—especially destructive behaviors—may change, but the "tendencies," even with

vigilance and the acceptance of coexistence, are ingrained and, at the level of character, are highly unlikely to change. So . . . coexistence provides a means for a healing outcome to develop despite the ongoing presence of what, left to its own devices, could still ultimately destroy one. *This fact: that one can achieve a level of "healing" in the presence of the "poison" is big news.*

(8) *Healing from, or* ***with****, the Energy.* It's easy to personify Addiction Energy as, first, last and foremost, a categorical foe. It seems like something we're always dealing with, and there's always hell to pay if we don't. And yet . . . this may not be the whole truth, for, if one drills down deep enough into the depths of Addiction Energy, one finds just . . . *ENERGY.* The "Addiction" part of "Addiction Energy" suggests that, in its origins, what starts as *ENERGY* in a raw, primal sense—an energy of vitality containing seeds of creation, destruction and renewed creation, without which life would not be possible—becomes tainted, twisted and skewed into a direction *of negative outworkings only.* What this reality (if it is true) suggests is that as we engage with Addiction Energy in a conscious way, through (as previously mentioned) becoming *reconciled* to its presence and actively accepting the responsibility to *co-exist* with it, *Addiction Energy itself starts to change.* Our own healing, meager at the outset as it may seem, may, in some way, be mirrored by what Addiction Energy itself is undergoing on "its end." There is no absolute proof that this is the case, but there *is* anecdotal evidence of this dynamic. For instance, in coming to grips with Anger and Rage Addiction (one form of Behavioral Addiction), engaging with the phenomenon of triggering which is such a

characteristic of this addiction (and so many others) via a technique called the *Self-Pact*—in which the *ENERGY!!* of triggering is harnessed to facilitate inner journeying—has clearly revealed that *the destructive nature of Addiction Energy, when engaged in this fashion, can recast its role from destroyer to guide and teacher.*[39] This hopeful discovery makes real a possibility that "healing," so to speak, may, in the fullness of time, be a two-way street. *Even the fact of anecdotal evidence that Addiction Energy, under certain circumstances, can recast itself into serving a constructive role, is big news.* The remaining entries regarding "healing" possibilities are all built on this dynamic of cooperative (and co-operating) engagement between a person bedeviled by an addiction (behavioral or substance-based) and the Addiction Energy that underlies and fuels it.

(9) *Coming to terms with the Energy (to good purpose always).* This level of possible healing is the product of a growing,

39. This has been the reported experience of approximately two dozen individuals who, over a period of six years, have used the *Self-Pact* as a means of intentionally engaging with the energy of "triggering"—so characteristic of Anger and Rage Addiction (and many other forms of addiction, as well)—as a facilitator of "inner voyaging." My book *Anger & Rage Addiction and the Self-Pact: New Lights on an Old Nemesis* (2013, Four Rivers Press. fourriverspress.com) presents a deep exploration into this form of addiction, and sets forth in careful detail the constituent elements of the *Self-Pact,* along with how it is used, and what it can lead to. Though originally worked out specifically for Anger and Rage Addiction, the *Self-Pact* would appear to hold promise in addressing the triggering phenomena so prevalent among addictions generally. As of this writing, research into the Self-Pact's possible efficacy in working consciously with the triggering aspect of Addiction Energy as it manifests in other Behavioral Addictions (and chemically-based ones, as well) belongs to the future.

"conscious" relationship with Addiction Energy. What originally commenced as a grudging recognition that Addiction Energy is in the mix of what comprises us "for keeps," followed by realizations of certain milestones along the path of reconciliation and coexistence, continue to evolve into experiences of mutual benefit. "Right to exist," as endorsed and supported by *both* poles in this continuum: self and "other" (Addiction Energy) gives rise to increasing familiarity with Addiction Energy on our part, and, presumably, a greater familiarity with us on the part of Addiction Energy.

(10) *Coming into proper alignment with the Energy!! ("owning" it).* This potential for healing (and the final two entries to follow) hint at longer-term possibilities as to what healing from, and *with*, Addiction Energy *may* mean. In truth, it is, at this point, largely (but not completely) uncharted territory. But . . . given that Bill W. (A.A.'s co-founder) dared to take a flier on codifying the "Promises" for the A.A. "Big Book" at such an early stage in his own recovery, here are a few admittedly visionary possibilities of what it—healing—*may* be all about.

"Coming into proper alignment with" carries the first hint of an *integrative* possibility between "me" and Addiction Energy. In "coming into proper alignment with," "I" enter, on a more or less continuous basis, into an experiential dialogue with Addiction Energy, and take note of what seems to reinforce positive, or "good purpose" outcomes, and what doesn't. There is a sense that Addiction Energy, in more consciously relating to "me," also has it's own tally to make as to what "works" for it and what "doesn't." Where "proper" alignment occurs—at first situational, rather than steady-state—there is a feeling of the "joining" of consciousnesses, awareness and intention. This is experienced as a mutual reinforcing of a bond that has been established between "us," leading to episodes of mutual benefit. *"Proper alignment" is an "energetic" experience, rather than a purely intellectual surmising.* There is dynamism to this flow of Energy, which, depending on the sensitivity—and evolving neurology—of the individual, may be accompanied by a feeling of physical embodiment (propagating chills, tingles, energy rushes, et al.). The sense of "both" of "us" lining up on the same side of a situation, or a plan, or an "issue" is very reinforcing—and feels wonderful. Momentarily (and maybe longer), conflict is gone.

(II) *Coming into proper dis-alignment with the Energy ("disowning" it).* No successful "marriage" grows without conflict. The essence of coming "into proper dis-alignment with" means that a certain amount of disharmony and friction are part and parcel of continuing to relate to Addiction Energy or (taking the part of Addiction Energy) Addiction Energy's continuing to relate to "me." There is even a possibility, hearkening back to the "possession" way of looking at things, that Addiction Energy, or some aspects of Addictions Energy, are truly foreign, or alien, and (theoretically at least) have no right to be present in the mix at all! *While I see this as unlikely, this cannot be completely ruled out as a possibility.* For instance, it is of more than passing curiosity that in the Lord's Prayer, probably the most frequently recited prayer within Christendom, the following line appears: " . . . and lead us not into temptation . . ." Without getting deeply theological, it's enough to mention that *the perceived need* for the line "and lead us not into temptation" to be included in this prayer indicates that codified in the wording of an appeal to a presumably loving God is the fearsome possibility that "God" might just be, under certain conditions, *capable* of "leading (me) into temptation." Applying this logical inference from that line from the Lord's Prayer into the addiction realm, it is always possible that a growing relationship between "me" and "Addiction Energy" could misfire, as much because of Addiction Energy as of "me." Addiction Energy, then, and the relationship forged with it, can never, even in redeemed condition, be unconditionally held up as the unquestioned "gold standard" regarding morality, ethics, "correct behavior," and traveling the road to true bliss in this life (and the hereafter).[40] To "work," a relationship is constantly recalibrating to the ever-evolving and changing needs, priorities, preferences and "certainties," that, in any given moment, may be prevailing for both parties, and then (for either) can be gone in the next. One should never be shy about disowning what does not, or does no longer, feel right, either in one's gut, or in one's heart of hearts.

(12) *Coming into proper* **resonance** *with Addiction Energy (becoming aligned with, and increasingly at one with, the underlying energy and vitality of Addiction Energy—the ENERGY!!).* "Alignment" is the act of being "in alignment with"—lined up with (so to speak), or congruent—and "dis-alignment" is the act of consciously moving out of alignment with a boundary—

40. Or otherwise . . . "trudging the road of happy destiny." (A.A. Big Book, page 164.)

an act of becoming intentionally separated from it. However, "*coming into proper resonance with*" is *neither* intentionally aligning oneself with, *nor* consciously dis-aligning oneself from, a certain kind of positional attitude or orientation relative to a border or boundary of some sort. *Resonance, rather, is the transmission of energy through some kind of medium (as in air, water, "spirit," and so on), and the effect that that transmission has on those who are attuned to a wavelength that can both receive and send it.* Resonance is not an intentional, or "willed" experience. It is a phenomenon in which a source of transmission meets with receptivity by a receiver of that transmission. "Resonance" is felt—embodied. Unlike "coming into alignment with," or "coming into dis-alignment with," it is not a strategic undertaking. Rather, it is an *experience*—often arising spontaneously—of recognized, and felt, *connectedness . . . sameness, even. . .* maybe even *kinship. Resonance* is bi-directional. To feel resonance is to know relatedness on a very intimate level, and to realize that *one is also becoming known* ***by*** *that "other level." To feel the resonance of the energy and vitality underlying Addiction Energy is to recognize oneself in that Energy—as part and parcel of it, not as someone or something apart from it.* In those moments of resonance with the energy and vitality underlying Addiction Energy, one experiences intimations of a deeper unity and harmony than words can possibly capture and convey. One is both reached by the energy of transmission, and, simultaneously, via resonance, the transmission is re-radiated back to its source, *and received there.* The sureness of "right relation," in which, at least in moments (and possibly for longer) Addiction Energy and "I" are one—the experience and recognition being *both* a product of a redemptive journey that has been traveled by *both* of us—the *Energy!!* and "me"—*both* fulfills, at one level, a kind of destiny, and hints at recognitions yet to surface and adventures yet to transpire in an unfathomable "future." *Somewhere in this experience of resonance is the knowing that one inhabits a complete, sustained abode.* It's something to lend a smile of recognition to, and it carries an experience of being inviolably, inwardly *secure.*

(13) *Encountering The Unknowable.* As a last offering in the "healing" direction, in the manner of a small benediction, I include here an excerpt from a passage (Passage 64: The Unknowable) from one of my earlier books entitled *The Living Oracle: Wisdom & Divination for Everyday Life.* This book was written over twenty years ago, as I was making my slow, painful way through mid-life transition, which involved the irrevocable, irretrievable loss of much in my prior life that I had come to hold dear. The book was an attempt to acknowledge, and honor, the ancient tradition of consulting sacred, oracular texts for the purpose of gaining divination, insight and, most importantly, *wisdom.* My hope is that the words which follow hold some useful resonance that can inform your own odyssey of healing, both on the personal level and, if it is your calling, within the healing professions, as well, and sustain you as you go about this challenging work on both planes. I offer it to you in the earnest wish that many blessings await you as you expand your work with addictions, now to knowingly include seeing, and working with, Behavioral Addictions of *all* kinds. I also offer it to you as a "fellow traveler" on the path (sometimes,

in self-help land, referred to as being "just another bozo on the bus"). May many others come to benefit from the healing that reaches you.

The Unknowable

The Unknowable is that which cannot be known. It is the ground of being itself. It underlies and envelops everything, but resists all impulse to be known in its native purity. It can only be sensed through its myriad manifestations, of which your life is one. As you come to know yourself more, you will draw nearer to it. Rest assured, the Unknowable knows you absolutely . . . Wherever your unknowns are, walk with care and keep your ear to the ground. Prepare to be surprised—astonished even, and hit blindside sometimes. It is the Unknowable's way of keeping you loose, and teachable. No premature fossilization for you! The Unknowable reminds us that Divine guidance can use any person, and any pathway, at any time, to reach us. In making room within your life and your soul for the Unknowable, you honor Universal intention. We are drawn and held to its bosom, and nurtured at its breast. Against the backdrop of the Unknowable we are all as wide-eyed infants, encountering, in each and every ever-present moment, a new lifetime in all its immensity, so bright and shining.

It has been said the psychotic drowns in the same ocean in which the mystic swims in delight. You know what this means. The Unknowable for you no longer holds peril; it is the ladle of being which stirs up your soup. It gives you life in all its inscrutable complexity, tests you in countless, mostly unforeseen ways, obliges you to make decisions when you feel ill-prepared to do so, and breathes its life through you as you breathe yours. Acknowledging the Unknowable will create life anew for you at every moment. And in the end, you will make it home to Ithaca.[41]

---

41. Excerpt from Passage #64, "The Unknowable," from *The Living Oracle: Wisdom & Divination for Everyday Life* (Four Rivers Press: 2009. fourriverspress.com)

Appendices

APPENDIX ONE

About Tolerance

Here's the deal on Tolerance, presented both as comprehensively and concisely as possible: Our bodies are miraculous, neurological, biological, biochemical entities. Independent of conscious intention by the body's presumed occupant—"you" in your body and "me" in my body—our bodies are always active, in the absence of conscious interference, to achieve and maintain stable functioning. When "I" decide I want to get high, drunk, aroused, "lit," "hammered," "wrecked," etc., I take something or do something to "get me there." From the body's standpoint, however, what I'm taking or doing to get "lift-off" is toxic; it throws the body's neurology and biochemistry out of stasis—out of stability. From a purely biological and biochemical standpoint, that is what "getting drunk," "getting high," "tap-dancing on moonbeams," "getting sotted", "getting hammered," "getting wrecked" is all about.

Our bodies, in their age-old, inherited wisdom, don't like being shoved out of stasis, and they immediately try to counter—counteract—via assimilation, digestion, dilution, metabolization, neutralization, expulsion (excretion) the "toxins" that have entered the body (or been created in it), along with the experiences of disequilibrium they have given rise to. In other words, whatever conscious intention to get drunk or high may be in play, the body, in its ancient wisdom, fights it absolutely.

Here's where the plot thickens: Given recurrent episodes of

being bombarded with toxins—alcohol, mind-altering drugs, and experiences that unleash a bevy of reactive neurotransmitters and adrenalin—*the body's remarkable neurochemistry increasingly comes to find a way to establish and maintain a degree of stability* ***in the presence of the toxin(s).*** As this trend of establishing and maintaining functionality in the presence of the toxins (either substance-based or activity-based) becomes more grounded and established, *the biochemistry of the body comes to regard the* ***presence*** *of the toxin as its "new normal"—as its basis for more normal functioning. It (the body) comes to accept, after a fashion, the presence of the toxin.*

The essence of TOLERANCE is twofold:

(1) Once this *new* basis of stasis—stability in the presence of the toxin—has been established, when conscious intention—the "you" and "I" in our respective bodies—wants to "get high," it takes much more toxin (either chemical or "acting out") to knock the neurology and biochemistry sufficiently out of whack so that a "high" can be experienced. The body initially still fights the disequilibrium and, as it gradually masters the trick of achieving stable functioning under these conditions, it takes an ever-increasing onslaught or inundation of consumption or indulgence to "do the trick."

(2) Here is where TOLERANCE gets really nasty: A new, ever-present and potentially lethal change now comes into play. As "getting high"—consciousness's goal—is thwarted more and more by the body's imperative to maintain functionality, and the body's ability to do so in the presence of the

toxin continues to increase, "getting high" (of whatever stripe) becomes less and less possible, and then, finally, no longer possible. The body's biochemistry and neurology have come to assert their mastery so completely that they "assume" that the toxins will *always* be there in the body; *they have now come to regard the* ***presence*** *of the toxins as their "new normal"—the necessary milieu in which they now maintain the functionality of the body. And then, finally, in order to maintain functional stability, the body's biochemistry and neurology come to* ***require—rely upon—completely,*** *the presence of the toxins.*

This is end-stage addiction, because the new danger is: ***If the toxin(s) (compounds or behavioral "acting out" activities that have toxic impact on the body, soul and psyche) are eased, their cessation = the onset of the neurology's and biochemistry's now being "whacked" out of functionality.*** *This form of being "whacked" is called "withdrawal," and, at this late stage in the progression of TOLERANCE, it is critical, dangerous and sometimes fatal.* While stability was, once upon a time, easy to maintain in a non-toxified body, those days are long gone. A suddenly "detoxifying" body has an even greater deleterious impact on neurological and biochemical stability than did the original experiences of getting drunk and high prior to the body's becoming acclimated to the presence of the toxins.

A person who is this far down the line in an addiction no longer uses/abuses/indulges to "get high." That's now ancient history. The new reality is that it's all about keeping withdrawal away and at bay—keeping enough "toxin," whether administered by chemistry or behavior, in the body for it to remain functional.

Such is the grim, nasty hook of tolerance.

APPENDIX TWO

A.A.'s Co-founders, Old-timers, and the Question of 'Possession'

Here is a portion of the evidence that A.A.'s co-founders and old-timers were taken up with the question of Possession as it may relate to alcoholism. This evidence draws on some observations about use of grammatical constructions in the "Step One" chapter in A.A.'s book *Twelve Steps and Twelve Traditions.*[42] The chapter starts by quoting (as first published in the A.A. Big Book): "We admitted we were powerless over alcohol, that our lives has become unmanageable." Within this chapter, *active voice* grammatical constructions—implying that Addiction is *something that "I" do to myself*—and *passive voice* grammatical constructions—implying that addictions is *something that is done to me*—something to which "I" am subjected—are used a total of ten times. Of these ten usages, only three are in the active voice, and fully seven are passive voice constructions.

Here are examples of two "active voice" statements in this chapter: "It is truly awful to admit that, glass in hand, we have warped our minds into such an obsession for destructive drinking that only an act of Providence can remove it from us" (*Twelve & Twelve,* p. 21). "By going back in our drinking histories, we could show that years before we realized it we were out of control, that our drinking even then was no mere habit, that it was

42. There are several other mentions of *Twelve Steps and Twelve Traditions* (nicknamed the *Twelve & Twelve)* in this book. It is readily consultable online at: http://www.aa.org/pages/en_US/twelve-steps-and-twelve-traditions

indeed the beginning of a fatal progression" (*Twelve & Twelve*, p. 23). Here are two passive voice statements: "Our sponsors declared that we were the victims of a mental obsession so subtly powerful that no amount of human willpower could break it" (*Twelve & Twelve*, p. 22). "The tyrant alcohol wielded a double-edged sword over us: first, we were smitten by an insane urge that condemned us to go on drinking, and then by an allergy of the body that insured we would ultimately destroy ourselves in the process" (*Twelve & Twelve*, p. 22).

In consideration of these evidential snippets of text (among a number of others) it seems fair to conclude that the grammatical use of active and passive voices in the language of the "Step One" chapter of the *Twelve & Twelve* is not merely a rhetorical device. Rather, the selective use of active and passive voice constructions suggests that the question of whether addiction is self-wrought or, rather, visited upon one by an external agency—a form of possession—was engaging the minds of A.A.'s co-founders and early pioneers as a part of their *subjective* reality. As self-help initiatives have always preceded, and blazed a trail for, the subsequent professional field of addictions treatment, the dynamic interplay viewing Addiction as something that is self-inflicted vs. something that involves being possessed by an external agency warrants being more seriously considered in our era. One thing is certain: One aspect of Addiction Energy is the carrying and manifesting of the dynamics of possession.

APPENDIX THREE

Culture as Camouflage in the Development of Behavioral Addictions [43]

The culture in which we live and come of age inundates us with messages that shape, often subliminally, our list of desires. These desires are presented to us as what we are *supposed* to want, how we're *supposed* to behave, what constitutes "success," and so forth. Our personal sense of values, in the absence of any countervailing, corrective force, naturally gravitates to what the overall culture presents to us as who, and what, we should aspire to be and do. The cultural milieu is, by definition, a "collective" force, against which nascent, personal, individual sovereignty holds little chance of prevailing. Under the guise of "striving to belong"—to be one of the pack—regardless of whether "the pack" holds to a conservative orthodoxy or to some stripe of self-styled revolutionary philosophy and mandate,

---

43. This chapter is written, in part, to honor the generation in which I came of age. It is dedicated both to the "hippie" end of the spectrum, consisting of many lost souls who didn't survive the era (as exemplified by two friends of mine, Chris Solomon, who fell victim to the drug culture in New York City, and was murdered there, and John Wolf, a ham radio buddy of mine, who fell tragically in love, enlisted in the Navy and died during basic training under suspicious circumstances), and to Vietnam War veterans whose lives were put on the line by a duplicitous government, many of whom died (including a school chum, a happy-go-lucky young man named Robert Larsen, who was killed in Vietnam), and others who survived the war, only to return home to an unsympathetic, even hostile civilian population. My heart goes out to those whose lives exemplified, articulated and suffered at, both ends of that spectrum.

those who are prone to Behavioral Addictions will find a ready array of ethics, morals and values that will serve to bolster the apparent legitimacy of such behaviors. A person prone to Behavioral Addictions can, and will, find plenty of places to hide out in any such milieu—such cultural camouflage—resting comfortably (or acting out with great gusto!) in the self-assurance that he or she is merely living out what is championed as "the way to go!"

What follows is a "snapshot" of one such cultural milieu. In its dynamic particulars, it is distinctive. *In its capacity to supply self-justifying camouflage for addictive acting out, however, it is not necessarily more or less enabling in this respect than any other cultural milieu or social phenomenon.*

This cultural milieu of which I shall provide a thumbnail sketch sets forth a bit of what it was like to be a "child of the 60s" (meaning: a child who came of age in the 1960s and early 1970s). This cultural milieu could well be called: The "Non-lethal STDs/Birth Control Pill/Civil Rights/Vietnam War/Hippie/Psychedelics/Massacre & Assassination Era."

Here is a list of ten characteristics and events from this era that helped to define it as a collective milieu for many millions of people:

(1) Antibiotics (Penicillin Gantrisin, and Tetracycline) had temporarily (although it seemed permanent at the time) made sexually transmitted diseases (gonorrhea, non-specific urethritis, syphilis, chlamydia, etc.) highly treatable. So the lethality (and culpability—proof of infidelity!) of having sex was seemingly eliminated—at least for the moment (roughly the twenty years

from 1960–1980.) No one was paying much attention, during this period, to antibiotic-resistant strains of gonorrhea that were already rapidly developing, nor to strains of the herpes virus that would start to develop and spread widely. In hindsight, it is clear that Hepatitis C was also around, but still unrecognized, and therefore not in the public consciousness. HIV was only an unseen mirage on the further horizon. The operative assumption of the era was that the potential lethality of sexual contact was permanently relegated to history.

(2) Birth control—"the pill." Approved for contraceptive use in 1960, "the pill" eliminated what had formerly been the inevitable risk, and often consequence, of sexual contact between women and men. The fear of unwanted pregnancy was gone.

(3) Combining the dovetailed effects of points 1 and 2, sex could be "risk-free": no lethality/no unwanted pregnancy. The typical restraints—the sexual mores as constrictors of indulgence—were gone. "Anything goes" from now on.[44]

---

44. In hindsight, what is so poignant about this 20-year period (1960–1980), when there appeared to be a lack of consequence for engaging in libertine sexual behavior, is . . . that this seemingly permanent immunity *did* last *only* 20 years! What felt (to many) like the arrival of the "promised land" of eternal sexual adventuring (no "commitment" required!), no unwanted pregnancy, consequence-free and guilt-free sex—rather than being the new reality, was, in fact, the outlier. With the arrival of highly drug-resistant strains of gonorrhea and herpes, the surfacing of HIV and the growing awareness of the prevalence, and long-term consequences of Hepatitis C, the "old" reality of "consequence," including lethality, that formerly attached to such explorations,

(4) Inequalities around civil rights and racial disparities along with racially directed violence resulted in the surfacing of a highly active, and visible, civil rights movement in the US. The March on Washington in August, 1963; the 16th Street Baptist Church bombing in Birmingham, Alabama in September, 1963 (which claimed the lives of four 14 year-old girls attending Sunday School) along with the events immediately following, the murder of three voter registration volunteers in the Mississippi in June, 1964, the Selma-to-Montgomery, Alabama voters rights march in March, 1965, along with many other initiatives, gave voice to a frothy brew of domestic rage and protest—all this also coinciding with the ramping up of the war in Vietnam.

(5) A highly questionable and increasingly unpopular war (the Vietnam War) continued to accelerate through much of this period. This war, and the duplicity with which the government pursued it, radicalized a generation of coming-of-age youth, leading to profound disillusionment with America and its governmental institutions, system of jurisprudence, etc. Radical, militant, and sometimes violent protest was the result.

(6) The "Summer of Love" (1967) unfurled in San Francisco. "Hippie"/psychedelic culture arose: "new morality," guilt-free sex," "free love," the rock group Crosby, Stills and Nash's message, "If you can't be with the one you love, love the one you're with."

---

reasserted itself with a vengeance. Indeed, the "new" would-be edenic reality turned out to be the anomaly—a fools' paradise—and the "old" reversion-to-the-norm reality of sex-related risk was the persistent, or real one.

Timothy Leary's message of "liberation" arose from the world of psychedelia: "Turn on; tune in; drop out."

(7) Combining points 3 and 6, hippie culture, championing the quest to re-engineer human nature—to create a society based solely on "LOVE!!" flowered into being (cue the psychedelic, Day-Glo lettering). The "Summer of Love" became a living enshrinement of this quest, role-modeling its ethos for the rest of a receptive, young—and vulnerable—population, both nationwide and international.

(8) Woodstock, August 15–18th, 1969. Two years after the "Summer of Love" in San Francisco seeded the radical drug/protest/drop-out culture, the signature event of the "hippie generation" took place in Bethel, NY. Countless thousands of the faithful converged on some farm fields, and steeped themselves in squalor, muck and mire, psychedelics and other drugs, amazing music, free-love, spiritual communion, mind-altering bliss and exhaustion. The assertion of the young, not-to-be-denied generation of radicalized protesters and truth-seekers exercised its coming of age as a *social* force.

(9) The atmosphere, especially among the coming-of-age generation, was one of tremendous permissiveness—especially permission to *experiment*. Anything goes (and went). The old cultural values of marriage, monogamy, conventional arrangements and livelihood were seen as stifling, imprisoning—as symptomatic of society's ills. A "guilty conscience" was a societal infection: an artifact—an introject—of a sick culture

(family, schooling/education, career norms, government, the military, organized religion) that fostered it and used it as a means of societal manipulation and control—to make the "sheeple" conform. All such mores were to be discarded. As a Schlitz beer ad from the era declared: "You only go around once in life so you've got to grab for all the gusto you can."

(10) Massacres and assassinations that hallmarked—pockmarked—this period included: the death of four 14-year-old black women (the bombing of the 16th Street Church in Birmingham, Alabama on September 15th, 1963—previously mentioned), John F. Kennedy (assassinated November, 22nd, 1963); Martin Luther King, Jr. (assassinated April 4th, 1968); Robert Kennedy (assassinated June 5th, 1968); Kent State University massacre of students by National Guardsmen on May 4th, 1970. Each of these events was a watershed happening that further alienated the upcoming generation from the society that had spawned it. The deaths of those enshrined as "liberal champions" (JFK and RFK, respectively), the death of the larger-than-life icon of successful, nonviolent civil rights struggles (MLK), and the death of student protesters—and *non*-protesters—on the campus of Kent State University at the hands of the American military all sent shockwaves through the American culture—especially youth culture. The latter event (the massacre at Kent State) hit closest to home for most people. The shock, horror, and disbelief that our own military could shoot down a population of United States citizens—students—brought forth cries of "They're killing our children!" "Our government has been reduced to a band of murderers!"

The dysphoric, alienating impact of these events, both individually and collectively, cannot be overstated.

All of these events (and so many more) came to define the coming-of-age generation, including, as well, those who had served in the Vietnam War, developed elephantine drug habits alongside their own disillusionment and dismay regarding what they both witnessed there and were obliged to do there. This disillusionment on the part of many American soldiers who served in Vietnam was further compounded when they arrived home to a largely unsympathetic, even hostile, domestic population which had grown weary of the war and the government that lied about it while continuing to push it. These alienated Vietnam War veterans brought their own drug addictions home with them, along with the pressing need to blot themselves out—to null out intrusive memories of the horrors they had both witnessed and participated in.

That is the brief presentation of some dynamics of one particular cultural milieu. All of what has been listed above produced an extremely powerful, pervasive and seductive subculture: an environment in which Behavioral Addictions (along with alcoholism and substance-based addictions), flourished and proliferated, under the camouflage of self-justified rebellion and its claims, as in "This is my birthright; I'm entitled to this," "I should want this," There's something wrong with me if I don't want this," "I must keep up with those who do want this" "If I fail to want this I'll fall prisoner to a conventional, 'neutered' existence," "Our government, social institutions and society at large are all corrupt; I condemn them and defy them," "I am a pioneer of new adventures into what being a human being really is, and means, finding honest, untainted, unstained values that truly matter and are not corruptible." This ethos, this dense cloud, hung in the atmosphere like a soaked blanket. It was palpable everywhere. It pervaded everything. Metaphorically, you could "cut it with a knife."

For anybody of a certain age attempting to get sober and clean during this era, it was against this coming-of-age climate-of-their-generation that the would-be sober/abstinent alcoholic/drug addict had to struggle in order to find a new life, value—and identity—in recovery. This volatile tide, drawing one into deep-immersion, self-righteous, self-indulgent adventures and experimentations of all sorts, was fiendishly difficult to swim against if one were to attempt, from the active addiction standpoint, any kind of recovery.

For many, to get clean and sober in this period seemed tantamount to becoming compliant with the very society that was responsible for all the evil—a form of "caving in" and "selling out." For them, it was inconceivable that getting clean and sober could be seen as "neutral space" in the culture wars, and that A.A. and N.A. took no side in the "right vs. wrong" of societal mayhem, having only an interest in helping alcoholics and drugs addicts, of *any* cultural persuasion, and from *any* point on the cultural continuum, get clean and sober, and into recovery.

Here is the takeaway from all this:

In summary, it is likely that each generation, notwithstanding geographical, demographic, cultural, sub-cultural, societal, political, geo-political and technological differences, has its own seductive, culturally reinforced worldview—

its own “new normal”—replete with internally consistent, compelling, self-reinforcing logic and justifications, in which, for those who are vulnerable, a new crop of addiction manifestations, including Behavioral Addictions, can take root and flourish, well hidden in and amongst such ready-made cultural camouflage.

Bibliography of Cited Works

Anonymous. *Alcoholics Anonymous.* New York, NY: Alcoholics Anonymous World Services, Inc., 2001.

Anonymous. *Twelve Steps and Twelve Traditions.* New York, NY: Alcoholics Anonymous World Services, Inc., 1997.

Augustine Fellowship. *Sex and Love Addicts Anonymous.* Boston: The Augustine Fellowship, Sex and Love Addicts Anonymous, Fellowship-Wide Services, Inc., 1986.

Currie, Ian. *You Cannot Die: The Incredible Findings of a Century of Research on Death.* Rockport, Massachusetts: Element, 1995.

Halpern, Howard. *How to Break Your Addiction to a Person.* New York, NY: McGraw Hill, 1982.

Johnson, William Oscar. "Marching to Euphoria." *Sports Illustrated* 53.3 (14 July 1980): 72–82.

Merriman, Stephen Rich. *Anger and Rage Addiction & The Self-Pact: New Lights on an Old Nemesis.* Amherst, MA: Four Rivers Press, 2013.

Merriman, Stephen Rich. *The Living Oracle: Wisdom & Divination for Everyday Life.* Boston/Amherst, Four Rivers Press, 2009.

Morgan, William P. "The Mind of the Marathoner." *Psychology Today* 11.11 (April, 1978): 38–46.

Peele, Stanton & Archie Brodsky. *Love and Addiction.* New York: Signet, 1975.

Scull, Andrew. "Nosologies: the future of an illusion," *Times Literary Supplement.* (18 May 2012): 14–15.

About the author

Stephen Rich Merriman makes his home in Western Massachusetts. He has found a loving community there. He lives with his wife Emily and daughter Eden, and two cats (Jasper and Goldie—both "rescues"), grateful, at his age, to have another family to love and learn from. He is semi-retired, and retirement from over three decades of clinical work in the addictions and dissociative disorders realms has freed him up to try to "give back," via writing a number of books which address both areas of human affliction along with other topics. These books present the best that has come to fruition in him over this lengthy span of work. He enjoys teaching and training in his areas of experience. He also greatly enjoys a reprise of an earlier career—that of jazz pianist and composer. He is grateful for the many blessings that have come his way.

The text for this book is set in Caslon 11/15
Printed on 50lb acid-free cream stock

Book designed by James McDonald
The Impress Group
Northampton, Massachusetts
jamesmcdonaldbooks.com

www.ingramcontent.com/pod-product-compliance
Lightning Source LLC
Chambersburg PA
CBHW032044040426
42334CB00039B/1231